Miami, You've Got Style

Miami, You've Got Style

A Golden Girls Zine

by Scott **and** Zach

Lovingly created in Portland, Oregon, 2008 and 2009.

Nerdlingerly dedicated to Larry Wall, Linus Torvalds, Stan Lee, and Frank Castle.
Dedicated to my darling Renee, the only remaining link I have to humanity...and to Sassy & Cleo, the only things stopping me from killing every single one of you.

To Shigeru Miyamoto, Gary Gygax, Gene Roddenberry and Richard Garfield.
For reals dedicated to my girlfriend Allison, for putting up with all my bullshit.

MIAMI, YOU'VE GOT STYLE: A LITTLE GOLDEN GIRLS BOOK

5th printing November 2013

Published by bunny project international

Visit us at miamiyouvegotstyle.com

Table of Contents:

Preface   xi

Introduction   xiii

Map   xvi

Episode I: The Engagement   1

Episode II: Guess Who's Coming to the Wedding?   6

Episode III: Rose the Prude   11

Episode IV: Transplant   18

Episode V: The Triangle   24

Episode VI: On Golden Girls   34

Episode VII: The Competition   42

Episode VIII: Break In   50

Episode IX: Blanche and the Younger Man   57

Episode X: The Heart Attack   62

Episode XI: The Return of Dorothy's Ex   64

Episode XII: The Custody Battle   68

Episode XIII: A Little Romance   72

Episode XIV: That Was No Lady   78

Episode XV: In a Bed of Rose's   82

Episode XVI: The Truth Will Out   87

Episode XVII: Nice and Easy   94

Episode XVIII: The Operation   98

Episode XIX: Second Motherhood   106

Episode XX: Adult Education   113

Episode XXI: Flu Attack   119

Episode XXII: Job Hunting   123

Episode XXIII: Blind Ambitions   127

Episode XXIV: Big Daddy   132

Episode XXV: The Way We Met   135

Endnotes   139

I have to say what I feel
Miami has so much appeal
A great place to get a seafood meal
Miami,
Miami, Miami, you've got style
Blue skies, sunshine, white sand by the mile
When you live in this town each day is sublime
The coldest of winters are warm and divine.
Miami, Miami, you've got style
Blue skies, sunshine, white sand by the mile.
There's ball clubs and night clubs, all within reach
Dance the samba till morning, then lie on the beach
Each view is a postcard, each day a great time
Cream of the crop, it's the top of the line
Miami, Miami, you've got style
Blue skies, sunshine, white sand by the mile.
Miami, you've got style!

Miami, You've Got Style

Disclaimer #1

This is not a perfect world. If it were then Estelle Getty would still be alive, I would eat ice cream sandwiches at every meal, and this zine would be in color. We spent a long time agonizing over the decision on whether springing for color was worth it. We feel that you lose something vital when these glorious outfits are viewed in black and white. Plus a lot of our comments just don't make sense. Unfortunately it proved to be just too expensive; color would quadruple the cost of the zine. But don't despair! On our website we have made available to you a color pdf of this zine so you can enjoy their outfits in the pristine rainbow of their magnificence. Just go to www.miamiyouvegotstyle.com/ggzine and behold the pastel-colored splendor!

Disclaimer #2

In the interest of funny humor and joke creation, a number of "jabs" have been thrown towards the community of senior citizens [old people]. While some of these jokes are actually facts juxtaposed to facilitate humor [IE, old people actually DO want to steal our youth away from us], many of them are just fabrications. Fabrications to try and make light of actual issues that are concerning us. It's a coping mechanism, and old people are unfairly bearing the brunt of the dark side of it. For this, we apologize, and hope that any old people reading this zine will realize that we do not hate them.

Psyche!

Preface

The golden girls saved my life.

A lot of people throw around statements like, "the BLANK saved my life", and it's usually as frivolous a thing to say as the word "literally". You know, the overuse of "literally"[1]? Anyway, The Golden Girls saved my life...and here's how.

Scene: 5th grade...a crusty bedroom littered with comic book archival tools (but never comic books...those were all neatly filed away).

When I was a young man I used to play sick in order to stay home from school and watch daytime TV. My dad is sort of a "gadget guy", and I've benefitted from this my entire life by making the best of his hand me downs. During this time of my life I was making the best of some old black and white TVs. I'd lay in bed for HOURS watching reruns of "All in the Family", "Little House on the Prairie", "Degrassi Jr. High", and "The Golden Girls". At one point I remember wondering if I suffered from insomnia, because I would LITERALLY (<-- used properly) stay up until 4am watching television. Those were good days. ANYWAY, so, sometimes if my 4am sessions spiraled out of control, I would pretend that I was sick the next day in order to avoid school (and to be able to catch the 11am showing of The Price Is Right). I very clearly remember waking up one day and debating whether or not to pretend I was sick in order to catch the last part of a two part GGirl episode. I believe it was "Golden Moments pt. 2", from the 3rd season, but I can't verify this. So...I was on the fence with it. It was one of those groggy wake up moments where millions of details are weighed in a very short amount of time, I was desperately grasping at any consciousness I had in my brain to guide my decision. I DID feel a little sore, and my stomach hurt a bit.... but back in those days I was eating about 2 pounds of Red Vines a day, and chasing them down with a 6-pack of Mt. Dew...so physical pain was the price of admission. I remember a peace washing over me...as Rose's matronly voice quietly whispered, "go to sleep, honey". I moaned something to my mom (who is/was a very good mom...and would not give her "A" student children grief about some missed school), and went back to bed. When I woke up, I was doubled over in pain. My Red Vine stomach had suddenly turned into a cauldron of nails.

I'll long story short the rest of this one. My appendix was moments away from bursting. What began as a "play sick" day to catch a GGirls two-parter quickly turned into surgery (and would be followed up later by MORE surgery, he knicked my colon). If GGirls hadn't been the quality program that it is...I may have caught the bus that day, and had to fight with an impotent public school district over the severity of my illness. My life was on the line, and the Golden Girls guided me to safe harbors. Thanks ladies...thanks for everything.

Additional Thanks To:

Mom, Dad, Allyson, Garrett, Bartles, Ryan, Heather, Drew, Joe M, Joe M, Sarah, Emily, George, and Zach. Hey, thanks!

Introduction

Bea Arthur died this weekend.

Early on while writing this thing Scott and I discussed possibly sending copies to the Golden Girls. We decided that if nothing else we should definitely send one to Bea Arthur. At eighty-six years old, Bea was still working and still fucking funny. She never lost any of her wit, or her sense of humor about herself. She was always "my" Golden Girl. Smart, caustic, constantly exasperated at the world around her. I am not going to say she was a role model, but ever since I was little I have always wanted to be the Dorothy in a group.

I used to spend weekends at my dad's house. Saturday night we would sit around on old empty cable spool in the living room, playing draw poker for pennies while I watched Golden Girls and Starman and The Incredible Hulk and Airwolf and Simon and Simon and a bunch of other shows. I love those memories, and for that reason Dorothy will always be in my heart. I wrote this for you, Dorothy.

> Pink on pink translucent shoulderpads
> Back on the rack
> Beatrice Arthur's dead
> The bats have left the bell tower
> The victims have been bled

Red velvet lines the black box
Beatrice Arthur's dead
Undead undead undead
The golden girls file past her tomb
Strewn with time's dead flowers
Bereft in deathly bloom
Alone in a darkened room
The Maude
Beatrice Arthur's dead
Undead undead undead

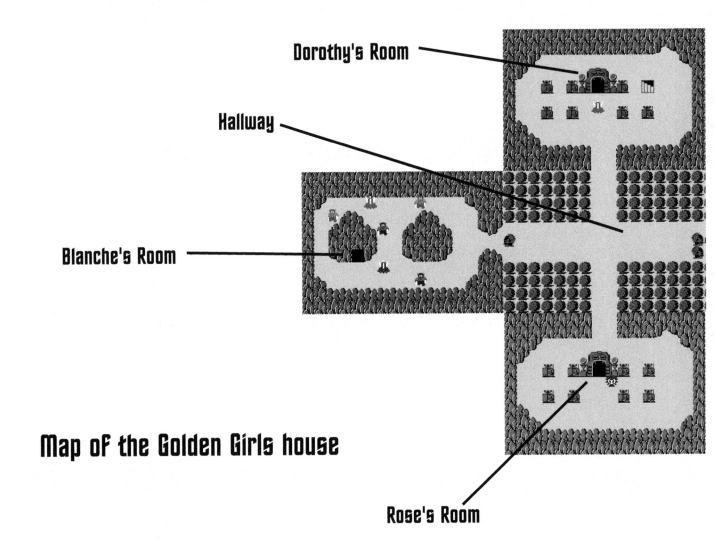

Dorothy's Room

Hallway

Blanche's Room

Rose's Room

Map of the Golden Girls house

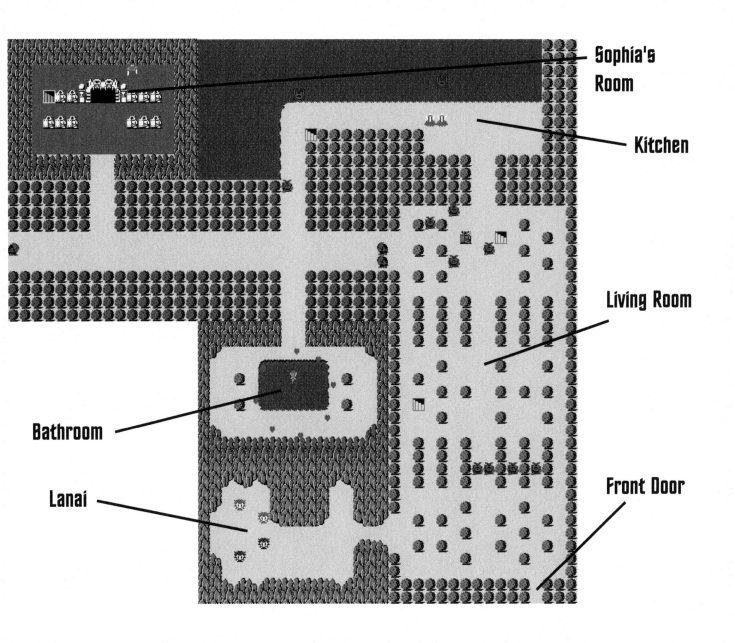

Sophia's Room

Kitchen

Living Room

Bathroom

Lanai

Front Door

Episode I: The Engagement

Dorothy's yellow shirt has made me powerfully thirsty for some orange juice. Blanche is one halloween mask away from being a "furry"[1].

If someone throws red paint all over the back of your fur coat then you need to get a new fur coat. Just cutting the back of your coat off is not an acceptable solution.

Blanche's skirt is making her upper body look like a slanty tree...rising from the sunkissed earth. I like to pretend that I am occupying the empty seat in this photo...

If you have a friend who wears ugly skirts that look like they were made from the curtains of a tiki bar, it is a good idea to have an intervention. Show your friend that you love them through lots of hand holding and group hugs so they realize it is not them that you are rejecting, just their tiki skirt wearing behavior.

This is a shoulder pad "hat trick"[2]. Also, this is the first episode of the Golden Girls...ever...and Dorothy is already committing acts of violence against her housemates.

Do not EVER try and wear bigger shoulder-pads than Dorothy. If you do she will fuck you up.

Yes Rose, I'm totally serious...your blue cowgirl shirt is FANTASTIC.

Are those buttons on her chest for pockets? It really doesn't look like they're for pockets. It looks like the entire lower half of the shirt can become detached. I think this is one of those shirts that you can wear if you want to be topless[3] but are worried that your shoulders might get chilly.

Sophia gets to go to the front of the line at all Deerhoof[4] concerts when she wears this outfit.

I wonder where that brooch came from? Do you think the wardrobe person went out and bought a new old-timey looking brooch, or did they go to an antique store? I like to think that a young female wardrobe assistant was recently given that brooch by her grandmother, and the grandmother made the brooch when she was herself a young girl. And the assistant tells her grandmother that it's beautiful, and she wants to have Sophia wear it on the show whenever possible so that as many people as possible can see how nice it is. So every week the grandmother watches Golden Girls, and sometimes she stays awake through it and sees the brooch and knows that her grandaughter loves her, but even if she doesn't she falls asleep smiling, with the tv on in the background and an old cat on her lap, purring. Cats are wonderful.

Sophia's American Apparel robe says "I'm flirty and confident"...her wicker "Urban"[5] purse says "I'm traditional...with an edge."

You know what's awful? When you can't find your glasses and you get all frustrated and are mean to your friends. Then later you realize they were around your neck the whole time. If this happens, make sure to apologize to your friends.

Rose's nightgown looks like a huge, expensive, impulse Kleenex that you would find in the checkout lanes of New Seasons[6].

I have not actually seen this episode, but I am pretty sure Rose just called Dorothy a cunt. That is why Dorothy is giving her such a dirty look. It's weird, because Rose is usually so nice. I guess because this is the first episode they don't really have the characters down yet.

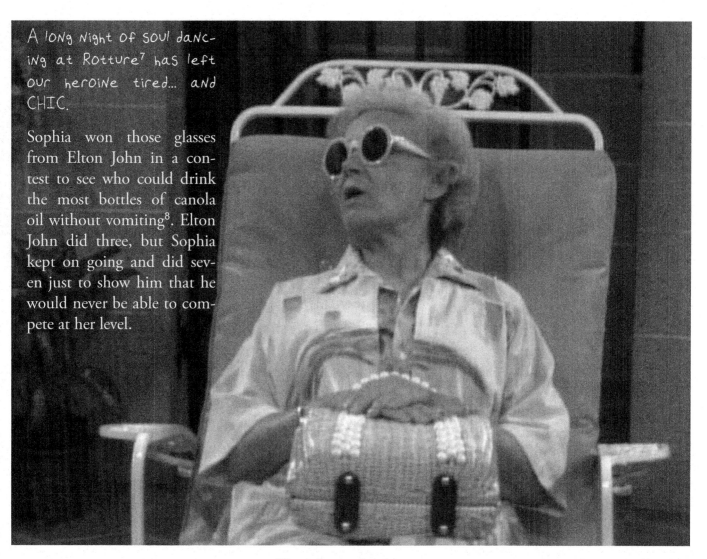

A loNg Night of soul dancing at Rotture[7] has left our heroine tired... aNd CHIC.

Sophia won those glasses from Elton John in a contest to see who could drink the most bottles of canola oil without vomiting[8]. Elton John did three, but Sophia kept on going and did seven just to show him that he would never be able to compete at her level.

Episode II: Guess Who's Coming to the Wedding?

This plunging V-neck can only benefit from the awkward placement of these polka dots.

In order to make the dots for this sweater the d6es[1] from countless Yahtzee sets gave their pips.

4-way pastel party in the kitchen! Good N Plenty purple, baby blue, mint green, and canary yellow. Magnificent. And look, they are rolling what appears to be cocaine into small doiley pouches adorned with lace flairs.

Sophia is angry because Dorothy bought tulle to match all of their outfits except hers (Tulle is that fabric they are wrapping the stuff in by the way. If you would like to know more about it, go back in time and arrange for you mom to own a craft store[2] when you were a little kid).

Sophia rocking a big old corsage. There aren't a lot of occasions to wear corsages so if you are going to wear one make sure it is big enough to count. As Sophia demonstrates, if your corsage is not at least 80% of the size of your head you might as well not even bother.

Don't be embarrassed about your garish pearl necklace, Blanche. Sophia's is way more elegant and understated. Rose's is timeless and stately. It's totally fine that yours is really gross and looks like a Mardi Gras "show your boobs" prize.

The blurry background of this photo is NOT a hasty error ON the part of this zine...the camera shooting this footage literally diverted all of its lens power to try and soak in as much of this masterpiece as it could. That flower isn't pinned to her shirt, it's growing directly out of her heart.

See, this is exactly what I'm talking about. Dororthy's corsage is completely overpowered by her ugly pink shirt because it is only 60% of her head size. When ordering corsages for more than one person DON'T JUST GET THEM ALL THE SAME SIZE. Make sure each person sends you a measurement of their head in advance and have each corsage custom sized. I cannot stress this enough.

Episode II

It is like they were making a shirt, then they realized that it was two feet longer than it was supposed to be and ran out of buttons. So rather than have the shirt part of the garment go all the way down they just decided to have it be a dress at the bottom.

This looks like a dress that Cathy of the comic strip "Cathy" would wear...and I love this dress, for that reason. AcK! AcK! AcK!

At first I thought this was a dress, but on closer inspection I believe it might be a nightgown. Either way, I approve. They are considered the second and fifth best garments to wear while carrying a tray with a pitcher of iced tea. When you consider the large number of possible candidates they are both very strong contenders.

6p̂λïï  6p̂λïï

Sophia looks relaxed after her swim in the pool at the Ace Hotel[4]. There's no pool at the Ace Hotel you say? ...sounds like you've been flying coach.

This robe is ideal if you want to trick nearsighted people into thinking you are wearing a giant stethoscope.

Episode III: Rose the Prude

I'M NOT a lady. So, please UNderStaNd that this stateMeNt could be steMMiNg froM igNoraNce. But, I doN't see a strap oN that purse...aNd that MaKes it the sMallest aNd Most iMpractical storage UNit ever.

An early version of this episode had Blanche breaking into Fort Knox[1] to steal the Hope diamond. There was a scene where she is hiding against a wall of gold ingots and uses this dress for camouflage. They later wrote that out of the script but they forgot to change the outfit, so now she just looks out of place for wearing something this gaudy.

We talk about the clothes a lot...what about the furNiture? This looKs liKe hotel furNiture to Me. ChecK out those light fixtures...aNd yeah, that phoNe...!?!?

Look at that old phone! This is my least favorite type of phone. You don't yet have the convenience of having the buttons in the handsets and at the same time it is lacking the retro appeal of the rotary-style phones.

I don't recall the circumstances that illicitted this sort of response from our heroines... but judging from the fact that Sophia is the only one that is psyched about what's going on, I'm guessing that someone just brought the new Ratatat[2] album over.

You have to be careful when wearing vests. They are surprisingly exhausting pieces of clothing. Dresses and sweaters? Not so much! But vests! They will get you tuckered out every single time.

500 years later, this outfit (minus the flowers, unfortunately) would become the gold standard for "sporty tops" amoungst the Romulan Military.

It's an ugly dress and it makes me kind of sad to see Rose wearing it. But not sad enough for me to be able to think of something hilarious to say.

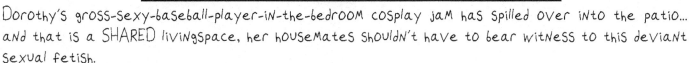

Dorothy's gross-sexy-baseball-player-in-the-bedroom cosplay jam has spilled over into the patio... and that is a SHARED livingspace, her housemates shouldn't have to bear witness to this deviant sexual fetish.

While shooting this episode Bea Arthur was simultaneously filming the movie "A League of Their Own", where she was working as Madonna's stunt double. It's true[3], you can look it up on IMDB. Anyways, one day shooting at the movie ran late and by the time Bea got to the Golden Girls set they didn't have time for a costume change, so they told her to leave the uniform on and they would just pretend that it was a hideous nightgown that was so ugly that if your mom saw you wear it she would feel guilty about not having an abortion.

Is it gross or sexist that I wish that all girls dressed like Sophia does? I KNOW it would get boring after a while, but I'll be damned if she isn't the greatest dresser that I have ever seen. I even like the croakies.

I spent two years living in Florida, a time in my life I both rue and lament. You know what I didn't see a lot of in Florida? In the middle of the day? People wearing sweaters.

Gryffindor welcomes you to the house of the Golden Girl!

I like this, but I am not sure why. Maybe because of the crest? Crests are pretty great. If I had a crest it would be a unicorn impaling a tyrannosaurs through the heart with its horn.

I think this is actually a nice outfit for Rose. The cuffs on the sleeves look uncomfortable...and her upper arms appear to be twice as wide as her lower arms...but, I honestly do enjoy this look for Rose.

If you look at the background you will notice both a painting of a vase and at the bottom of the frame you can just barely see the top of an actual vase. In the literary world we call this a metaphor.

80's jungle safari...put a martini glass in this lady's hand and point her to the nearest elephant gun[4].

It sort of looks like Rose is wearing a trench coat here. That would be neat, if Rose had her own show where she was a detective. It would be similar to Police Squad[5] I guess. That was a pretty good show. Or at least it was when I was twelve. I am scared to go back and watch it now for fear that it will not be nearly as good as I remember.

yŵí   yŵí

Rose is actually trying to seduce an elderly man in this photo...and the seduction is working, on ME. I don't even feel weird admitting that.

Damn, Rose looks pretty good here! I know Blanche is supposed to be "the hot one" but I think Rose is way more attractive. I also think she would probably be lots better at sex. Blanche strikes me as a very selfish lover but I don't get that vibe at all from Rose. I think she would be patient and kind and giving, and would never make you feel bad if you had a tough day and you're having trouble maintaining an erection.

For my money, this is the best shot of the entire season. Blanche in her elegant southern geisha gown...Dorothy in her Nightmare in Neverland nightgown...Sophia keeping it real in a Siccily thiftstore sleeping gown. Again, I find myself wishing that I was occupying that empty seat.

Thanks to the pioneering efforts of Dorothy and Sophia I expect Victorian bathing suits to make a comeback any day now.

Sophia isn't sure which of her totally modern (IE out of focus) photos to send into Vice Maga-zine[6].

Oh look, it is the brooch again! Somewhere the imaginary grandma I mentioned previously is smiling!

Episode IV: Transplant

When you are old and retired...finding, paying for, and then subsequently arranging flowers takes up like 40% of your day.

Alright, Blanche knows where it's at! Now THAT is a motherfucking corsage!

Blanche's "goldenrod" shirt seems to have been given the gift of life...and is using this gift to desperately try and get away from her.

Fashion tip of the day: If you have a piece of clothing and you think it looks okay but you want to make it more hideous, just add some bows to it because bows are awful. They are the fashion equivilent of Hitler having diarrhea on your favorite childhood toy.

They sure do have a lot of cups for just two people. Maybe it is so they will have a cup in each hand? One time I was working late at the hospital, and I was bringing back cups of water for me and another technician. On the way I saw a somewhat hot girl. She held the door open for me, and asked me if I was into double fisting. Now, I didn't realize this at the time, but apparently among you kids today double fisting can refer to having a beer in each hand and she was making a joke about that. I was unaware of this. I only knew of the old person definition, which is to shove fists into the vagina and anus simultaneously. The moral of my story is that I blushed and was sort of embarassed because of a misunderstanding.

I didN't SERIOUSLY start drinKing coffee uNtil I was liKe 23 or someThiNg. I was coNviNced that it sapped my immuNe system...aNd I was coNstaNtly depressed aNd just waNted to sleep aNyway. This dress is very slimmiNg oN BlaNche.

Dorothy is wearing a tuxedo shirt and nurse's scrubs, and I have no idea why this is so. Rose actually looks pretty nice here, I'm going to go out on a limb and call that a v-neck sweater...love it. Sophia looks like she accidently wrapped the bathmat around herself in a fit of confusion...but her cool, post-realization / pre-correction attitude towards the whole situation is enabling her to pull it off.

It looks like they are having fried chicken and grapes? I think that is a weird combination. It would be an acceptable combination for a picnic, but at no other time. This goes on my list of meals of disapproval.

Legitimate concern of mine: Old people have the ability to sap the youth away from people younger than 30 years old.

Cats are better than babies in every concievable way, and I don't understand you breeders at all. Although maybe I am being presumptuous. I suppose that blanket could be filled with adorable kittens. Adorable scottish fold kittens! And they would all be going mew mew mew! That would be so cute!

Yeah Rose, I too was surprised when Blanche quietly whispered to me that hoverboards[1] were real and that parents had lobbied lawmakers to make them illegal because they were perceived to be too dangerous for the consumer market. I too, was surprised. Check it out though Rose, Blanche is just lying in order to try and impress you.

When I was in middle school I was best friends with the son of the lead singer of Foreigner[2]. He had a really hot mom who was into lots of new agey stuff. I used to pretend to be sick, and then she would try to diagnose it with kinesiology[3] which I thought was the dumbest bullshit in the world for suckers but I totally went along with it because I liked having her touch my arms. I have no regrets about this. Anyways, the way Rose is touching Blanche, it reminded me of that.

This feels like it could be selling something in a magazine. This feels like what I imagine the TV show Project Runway feels like...but I have not seen this show.

She looks incredibly determined and purposeful. And also grey. I bet this is what Robocop's[4] mom looks like.

Let's say you and some friends all agree to wear matching cream colored collared shirts. If one of your friends forgets and wears a nightgown that looks sort of like a kimono instead, DO NOT try to make her feel better by putting on an ugly purple sweater over your shirt and pretend like nothing is wrong. She will still notice the collar, and your feeble attempt to cover up their faux pas will only make things worse.

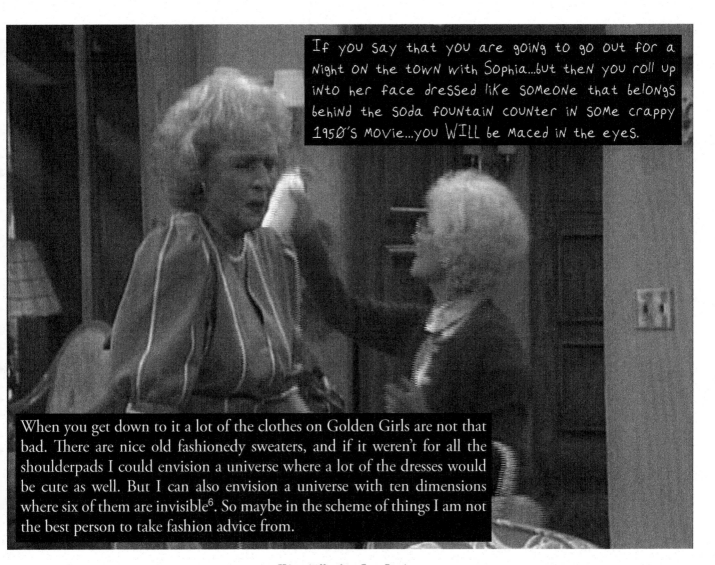

If you say that you are going to go out for a Night ON the tOwN with Sophia...but theN you roll up iNtO her face dressed like SOMeONe that belONgs behiNd the sOda fOuNtaiN cOuNter iN SOMe crappy 1950's MOvie...yOu WILL be Maced iN the eyeS.

When you get down to it a lot of the clothes on Golden Girls are not that bad. There are nice old fashionedy sweaters, and if it weren't for all the shoulderpads I could envision a universe where a lot of the dresses would be cute as well. But I can also envision a universe with ten dimensions where six of them are invisible[6]. So maybe in the scheme of things I am not the best person to take fashion advice from.

Episode V: The Triangle

Blanche has that "I have to go to the bathroom" / "I am a hollywood monkey who's trainer is purposefully scaring me in order to illicit a smile" smile that does not sit well with me. Move out of the doorway Blanche, I'm going to Sophia's room.

Possibly the darkest colored outfit to yet appear on this show. It is entirely appropriate that Blanche is wearing it as the darkness of this outfit mirrors the shadow that consumes her shallow, fickle heart.

This looks sort of like a nightgown, right? She's putting makeup on though, so it can't be. Check out the doorknob to the left, it could almost be mistaken for one of her earrings.

Always carry a mirror with you. Sure it's great for touching up makeup, but it will really prove its worth if you need to fight a gorgon[1].

Some old guy looking completely normal in a suit. I don't understand how one does this. I recently had an idea that maybe it would be nice to occasionally not still dress like a high schooler and to have some fancy type clothes. I am not talking about meeting the pope fancy. Just so that if I tried to go to a nice restaurant they wouldn't throw boiling water in my face before kicking me out. But whenever I put on nice looking clothing I think I look like a freak. Like I am wearing a costume that doesn't fit. I cannot fathom how every person who sees me is not whispering under their breath "Who the fuck does he think he's kidding?!". And I look at other dudes who are wearing shirts with buttons on them, and they look normal. Like they are supposed to be dressed that way. I don't know what is wrong with me, why I have such a problem with this.

The old men on this show are really gross looking...and highly sexual too...which is a source of neverending freakouts for me. When I get to be this age, I'm just going to sit around doing drugs and playing scrabble all day[2].

Dorothy unveils her plan for cleaning out a Vegas casino. Step 1) grab the money from the hands of the pitboss. Step 2) lay flat on the ground and completely disappear by blending in with the carpet patterns. In case you can't tell...I'm saying that her outfit looks like casino carpets!

I used to know this guy who worked at a crayon factory and one day it exploded and he was killed by being covered in searing hot wax and this is what he looked like when they found him. True story[3].

For my money, this outfit is the embodiment of Mervyns[4] in the early 90s.

Let's say you are staying in a hotel and you decide to steal the curtains and make a dress out of them. If you want to be able to pull off a dress like this, you need to strut. Carry yourself with pride. Own that motherfucker. Constantly hum that "I'm too sexy for my shirt" song[5] to yourself to put yourself in the right frame of mind.

I give her some credit for having a purse that perfectly matches her outfit. This is a frivalous move, but one that I have to give her credit for. Her SCARF though? Is she hiding an adam's apple under there?

Oh, they have a fireplace. This is not weird to me because when I lived in Florida there was a fireplace in every apartment I rented. Not something I really understood. Did I mention that Florida is the most horrible place in the world? If I have not mentioned it previously I would like to do so now. Florida is the womb from which is birthed a sorrow that will never die.

This looks like a pink karate uniform with pleats added to the front of it. KIYAP!⁶

They all seem to have a lot of nightgowns. Is it normal for people to have this many nightgowns? I have never worn one. Are you supposed to change them daily? Is there a stigma attached to wearing pajamas for two days straight like there is regular clothing? If we include contact information with this, feel free to write to me with your thoughts on this topic.

Could you imagine a life where you get to drink orange juice and coffee for breakfast every morning? It just seems like such a decadent and amazing way to start the day. My breakfast is literally just me snaking my head under the faucet and drinking some water.

It is no surprise that Dorothy is the Gryffindor[7] of the group.

Three pretty solid outfits in this shot. Excellent cardigan on Dorothy. Fantastic "action slacks"[8] on Rose. Decent shirt combos on the old dude over there...but I'm sorry to say that his plaid pants have snapped me out of the "liking plaid pants" phase of my life.

This guy is probably the greatest hero our country will ever see. Those pants are incredible and the fact that he matched his shirts to the highlights in them is even better. He wins seven nobel prizes for this outfit.

This is just the most comfortable fabric that a person can wear...and I want to live in a world where everyone can be a part of that.

This top would be way better if it was fleece. The fact that it is not totally ruins it for me. This is the kind of shirt that your mom had when you were a little kid and it is super soft, and when no one else was home you would sneak up to her room and put it on and enjoy the pleasant fluffiness.

Look at her...eyeing that empty glass on the table. She's like a laser-guided missle of orange juice dispersement.

I can't understand why all the orange juice manufacturers brag about having fresh-squeezed Florida oranges. Florida oranges are garbage. That would be like a hamburger company bragging about how their patties are made from all the worst parts of a cow. California oranges though, those are good. I love them so much I wish I was having sex with one right now.

Rose is seriously the most awesome character on this show, BY FAR. Awesome robe, check. Milk 'n oreos, check. Why is she still wearing her wedding ring though? I feel really sad about that. I'm sure it's just because she loves her dead husband and blah blah blah...but I wish she had some man happiness in her life now.

I have little to say about this besides mentioning that Oreos are pretty tasty.

Once again, Rose is a total vision of grandmotherly excellence. Are you kidding me with this apron?

Aprons! Where the hell are you!? I have been waiting years for aprons to take off as a fashion accessory! It is nice to see that at least Rose has my back.

OK! OK! Jesus Christ, Sophia...I'll go with sample A. Don't bite me...

While that cardigan is super cute, it carries with it a terrible curse that as long as you wear it you are forced to carry a plate in each hand. Also it gives you horrible status effects, but you can cancel that out by wearing a ribbon. Also also the curse will break if you wear it for two hundred and fifty five fights at which point it will turn into the Paladin Shield[9].

Miami, You've Got Style

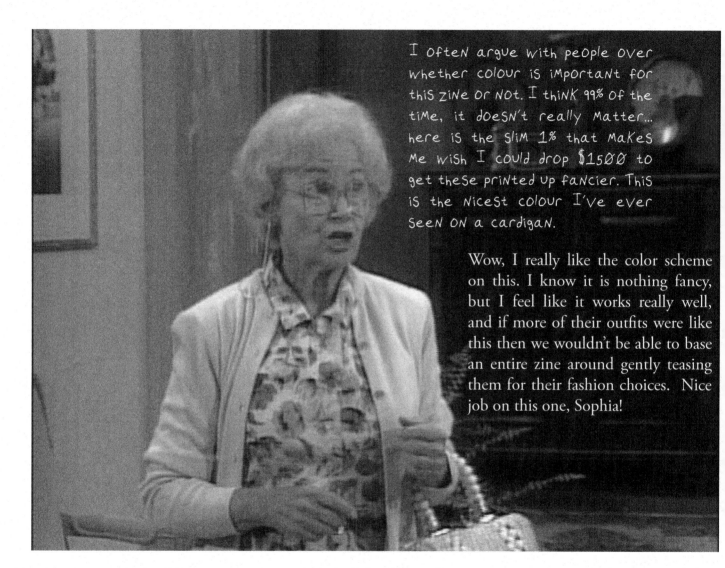

I often argue with people over whether colour is important for this zine or not. I think 99% of the time, it doesn't really matter... here is the slim 1% that makes me wish I could drop $1500 to get these printed up fancier. This is the nicest colour I've ever seen on a cardigan.

Wow, I really like the color scheme on this. I know it is nothing fancy, but I feel like it works really well, and if more of their outfits were like this then we wouldn't be able to base an entire zine around gently teasing them for their fashion choices. Nice job on this one, Sophia!

As opposed to this shirt, which made me throw up in my mouth a little.

Looks like someone scored big time at the Miami Goodwill. A purple and green wrangler shirt[10] on someone's great grandma? Yes please.

Double nightgown again...totally confusing to me. What happens when one of the Golden Girls has to go to the bathroom when they are wearing the double NG? It must take like 15 minutes to strip down, and frankly...I don't think these ladies have 15 minutes to spare under those circumstances[11].

She looks unusually good here. Maybe it is the color of the coat? I dunno. I know the wardrobe department on this show is racist against warm colors, but she should try wearing yellow more often.

Episode VI: On Golden Girls

Remember that show "Parker Lewis Can't Lose"[1]? Yeah, I loved it too. Anyway...the punk in the jean jacket would go on to be a regular character on that show. He is wearing this jean jacket at a time in history when jean jackets were beginning to lose their tough guy edge.

This kid stays up late, laying in bed, pretending he is the blue guy from Double Dragon[2]. Dude, you are way too old for this. Besides, Marian is all mine. Stay away from her.

I wonder how much laundry these women have to do! You aren't here right now to see it, but I'm throwing my arms up in confused frustration over this issue. They seem to wear at least four outfits during the course of their day. Morning - last night's nightgown...Afternoon - flowered dress... Evening - different flowered dress...Nighttime - new nightgown.

If you are old and you want to have a conversation with some young people and you want those young people to take you seriously, do not have that conversation while wearing the nightgown that Dorothy is wearing. It is the antithesis of young people taking you seriously.

I cannot tell where that chair ends and Sophia begins, and this is a further testament to her fashion greatness. Dorothy is writing a BOOK about what a great dresser Sophia is, and how it is a constant source of embarrassment in Dorothy's life.

If you are the type of lady who likes to trick people into thinking you are wearing a two colored scarf when really you are not, then I cannot highly enough recommend Dorothy's shirt to you. It is the height of scarf/shirt trickery.

This is an outfit that I would maybe wear... and that sort of gives me pause.

Blanche is distressed because someone just shot her clothes with a photoshop gun set to greyscale.

Based on some tv shows I've watched I feel like I have had far less casual sex than many other young people and I can't help but wonder if a large part of this has to do with me not drinking. I mean, Blanche is probably about to have sex and she's drinking, so it's obviously helping her. I dunno. I don't regret the life I've led but I sometimes wonder if things would be more fun if I had made more bad decisions.

Zip up the shirt...put on a helmet...paint the whole thing red...and Blanche is ready to stand beside Emperor Palpatine as a trusted body guard[3].

I am not positive, but I am pretty sure that the figure visible against the blue background near the top of that vase is a baboon version of Abraham Lincoln.

I endorse inside out clothing, but only for certain fabrics. Like velvet. I mean, the best part of velvet is how it feels, right? So why would you want to have all the fuzzy pleasantness on the outside? This coat however appears to be some sort of fleece, which generally feels as good on the inside as it does on the out. If you own this coat or a coat like it, you do not have my permission to wear it inside out.

I'M WRITING THIS IN MY UNDERWEAR...AND I'VE HAD THIS T-SHIRT ON FOR LIKE TWO DAYS...SO, I AM NOT ONE TO TALK...BUT I'M TALKING ANYWAY... DOROTHY, YOUR SHIRT IS INSIDE OUT, AND THAT IS LAZY.

Dorothy looks skeptical, but I have no doubts...Rose, your flowered dress is classy and I would be honoured to awkwardly hold a door open for you...and speak louder than I am comfortable doing while we discuss what things were like during "the war".

They always look like they have put so much effort into their appearance, but why do they do it? I can't help but be reminded of the head of the British POWs in Slaughterhouse Five[4], who stressed that taking care of yourself is the best way to keep their spirits up in light of a bleak existence. But in this case the women, like us all, are prisoners to their slowly deteriorating bodies and brief span on this earth. If you think about the futility of our situation it is sort of depressing, which is why I recommend that you not think about that and instead ponder why they have five plates for four people.

They're BOTH wearing double Nightgowns. How is this even possible?

Pastel nightgowns are the best kind of nightgown for reading several books at the same time. If you are doing this and trying to get away with wearing another kind of nightgown I don't even want to talk to you.

You could seriously replace the head of Sophia in this picture with the head of Roseanne Barr, and not have the picture look weird at all.

Sophia wore this shirt in an earlier episode. It looked familiar then, and I think I just figured it out. This looks just like the shirts Kim Jong-Il wears except it has a colorful collar. Also, she is wearing a bright yellow apron. Which might be a good look for Kim to adopt; Things always seem so dour over there, and I feel that a bright yellow apron might do a lot to lift the mood of the starving illiterate peasants.

I've never had an alcoholic beverage with my mom. She doesn't drink because "people just try and get the drinks to taste like juice, so why not just drink juice?" Hardcore.

Watch out Dorothy! There is a tiny elephant sneaking in on the right side of the frame and it is about to touch your boob!

Episode VII: The Competition

I'm calling it, right now...Blanche is my least favourite Golden Girl. She over-sells everything, and she looks like she smells like clothes from The Bins[1].

If you have to wear a shirt that has mismatched buttons make sure it is an ugly as fuck teal shirt so that people are too distracted by the rest of the shirt to notice.

Dorothy is dressed like Kevin Smith, post-1998. Shame on you, Kevin Smith.

Wow, that is such a good price for a Turkey Delight sandwich! I am tempted to invent a time machine right now just so I can go to this bowling alley and get one.

I count five distinct shades of pink in this photo. Pretty amazing. Does Blanche have some sort of bow made out of hair stuck in her hair? This is a waste of everyone's time.

Under normal circumstances I would criticize them for having light pink, salmon pink and bubblegum pink all in the same shot. However this fashion faux pas is COMPLETELY offset by the fact that the shield on Blanche's shirt is the exact same shape as the shields used in the Lego castle[2] sets.

If the clever person from the prop department that stole these bowling shirts is reading this zine right NOW...please get in touch with me. We have business.

Thank you Golden Girls for your tireless efforts to make black and pink an acceptable color combination. Radical cheerleaders everywhere owe you a debt of gratitude.

Believe it or not, this yellow/blue/red shirt that Rose is wearing is the outfit that she will SOON change OUT of, in order to go bowling.

Yeah, I'm really not sure about that shirt. It is like a horrible amalgamation of Ronald MacDonald and the Grimace[3].

It looks like she's wearing a really tall car...and her legs are in the place where the wheels would go. BILLOWLY.

I don't know about you but whenever I wear over-sized brown shirts it gets me in a pointing mood.

This is Dorothy's totally rad cosmic-wizard shirt. There are drawings of various space-centric things...and upon it are emblazen words like "planet", "comet", "Mars". Dorothy gets to skip the line at the Doug Fir[4] whenever she wears this out.

I realize that bowling is technically a sport but if you need to towel off afterwards you are doing something wrong.

I don't like to look at that as a hat. I like to approach it as if Sophia has finally lost her mind and has put a cereal bowl upon her head in a desperate attempt to get more attention. If Dorothy won't relent, Sophia will lift up her purse and reveal that she's wet herself. This is what I see.

Why don't girls wear hats that match their outfit anymore? You cannot deny that this outfit is fucking adorable. I am not such as asshole that I think all girls are just trying to look nice so that boys will notice them. But maybe some of the ones with really low self-esteem are? Girls with low self-esteem: wear cute hats if you want boys to pay attention to you.

Dorothy looks like she's ducking down low to enter that warp pipe in front of her. OH! Look out! It looks like the piranha plant[5] is coming out to bite you...I hate my life.

Dorothy always has her sleeves rolled up. I wonder if she has something wrong with her forearms? Maybe she has a disorder where her nerves are all messed up so that any sensation of touch that registers in her forearms is interpreted as pain. But if she is the case why doesn't she just wear shorter sleeved shirts? Why does she insist day after day to wear long sleeve shirts and then roll them up?

If Blanche didN't have that crisp lOOKiNg puff Of hair ON tOp Of her MelON, She wOuld lOOK EXACTLY liKe the bad guy frOM CaddyShack[6] iN this picture.

If you have not yet learned that gardening is supposed to happen in the ground and not on the table, then you deserve a disapproving lecture by Rose.

If this were aNy Super NiNteNdO gaMe featuriNg a guy with a SwOrd...aNd ROSe waS the guy with the SwOrd...She wOuld be charging up to "dO a Special" right NOW...aS iNdicated by the glOwiNg Nature Of her tOrsO.

This dress is a little too busy for me. I think it would look really nice if it was just the blue and the red, but the addition of the orange just turns into another one of their mundanely tacky dresses.

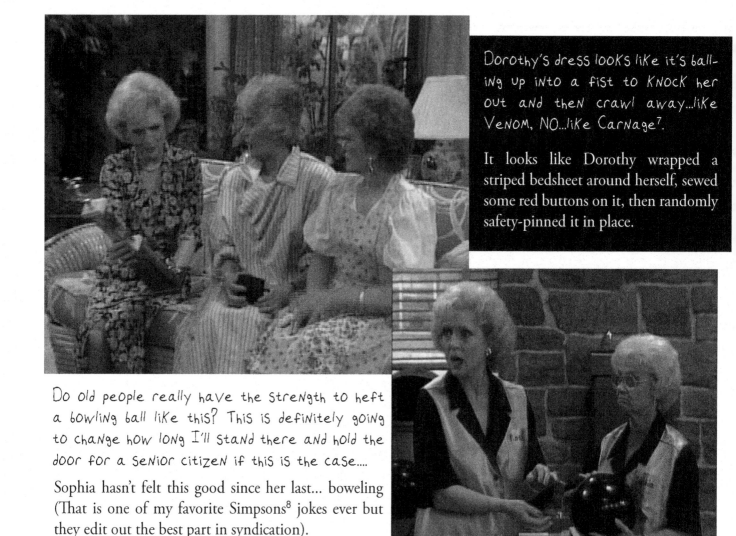

Dorothy's dress looks like it's balling up into a fist to KNOCK her out and then crawl away...like Venom, NO...like Carnage[7].

It looks like Dorothy wrapped a striped bedsheet around herself, sewed some red buttons on it, then randomly safety-pinned it in place.

Do old people really have the strength to heft a bowling ball like this? This is definitely going to change how long I'll stand there and hold the door for a senior citizen if this is the case....

Sophia hasn't felt this good since her last... bowling (That is one of my favorite Simpsons[8] jokes ever but they edit out the best part in syndication).

Could you imagine how awesome it would be to have this woman in your kitchen all the time... constantly cooking, and just sort of shuffling around with her purse[9]? Jesus Christ...sign me up.

I wonder what Sophia is making. Maybe some chili? Chili is pretty tasty after all. Then again maybe old people don't eat chili. This is an area where I admit I am woefully ignorant. I have very little knowledge of what seniors eat when real people aren't watching.

The Sisters of Mercy are opening up for Bauhaus and Christian Death[10]...and you know Sophia isn't going to miss this. Bonus goth points: her advanced age puts her closer to DEATH than anyone else at the show...BURN...except maybe Peter Murphy. DOUBLE BURN.

Holy crap that is a dark outfit. I cannot even see texture in it. Sophia is wearing a dress so black that light cannot escape it.

Episode VIII: Break In

Fact: IN this shOt, they are returNiNg frOm a MadONNa cONcert. 1985, "The VirgiN TOur". This meaNs that the GOldeN Girls alsO saw the OpeNiNg act....THE BEASTIE BOYS. Such a pleasaNt image fOr a persON tO pONder ON a quiet Friday Night...

I don't really understand why you would have the number pad for your security system on the outside of your house, but okay. I'm sure nothing bad will come of it.

Oh no! Because the number pad was on the outside it allowed hooligans to come into your house and make all your pictureframes slightly askew! And to make things worse Dorothy is wearing an ugly coat!

BlaNche wiNS the "best reactiON tO a breaK-iN" cONtest. SOphia just lOOKS liKe she's checKiNg Out a hOt seNiOr...ROse lOOKS liKe she's fed up with a NOisy tOddler...aNd DOrOthy lOOKS liKe she's just beeN bested iN a cONtest Of wits.

This is one of the better ties I've seen in my life. Woal, with stripes of gray and yellow. Actually, I like everything about this man's outfit...including his glasses. I want to date girls that dress like Sophia, so maybe that makes sense.

I wonder if there are clubs for old men who like to wear horrible jackets? Like, they all get together once a month and they bring old incredibly ugly coats that they might have grown out of and have a clothing swap meet thing and talk about what color ties might not match their jackets at all.

Rose looks like she's about to sock Blanche in the jaw.

If you have a security blanket and that blanket is made out of animal furs, then you better either be an eskimo or someone who is so rich that they wear a monocle 24/7.

Dorothy is in the middle of getting beamed up to the Starship Dentureprise.

I think Dorothy might have vomited all over her sweater? I understand that she is upset because someone broke into her house and made her pictureframes all slanty, but that is no excuse for such a lapse in hygene. Change your sweater or at the very least wipe some of the vomit off with a paper towel.

If you were ACTUALLY sick, you'd have a blanket over you right NOW. People don't stack up pillows like that without a blanket to top it all off. She is FAKING.

When the occassions of me being young and me having a fever coincided, I would lay on the couch all day and once in awhile my mom would bring me a pile of cool wet washcloths to put on my forehead. It was pretty great. Thanks mom!

Sexy baseball player fail.

Huh. For Dorothy that is almost scandalously revealing. And I suppose for Sophia too.

IN my first NSC sanctioned Scrabble tournament, I played against a lady about Sophia's age. She played CUNT on her first turn. It was intense.

Oh fuck yeah! Scrabble! I am pretty good at scrabble, mostly because I had a bet with my friend where he got to pee on me if I lost[1]. It was a powerful motivator.

It's like that young man I caught peeing on my house once said to me...."when you gotta piss, you gotta piss."

If I have one criticism for this outfit it is that her hat is not also pink. You really let me down on this one Rose.

This dress looks like something that I would place my glassware on while I wait for it to dry.

If you are going to wear a dress that looks like a bathrobe, then just go all the way and wear a bathrobe. You will be more comfortable and powerful people will respect you for your free-thinking ideas on fashion.

If this were the last thing I ever saw on earth, I'd be cool with it. I don't have a DESIRE to die right now, but I'd gladly die at Rose's hand.

Rookie fashion mistake: you accessorize robes with semi-automatics, not revolvers. Revolvers are for only nightgowns, while fully automatic handguns are best matched with one piece footsie pajamas.

It looks like they are burning a stack of books in their fireplace over there...

Wow, Phillip Seymore Hoffman looks awful here. I know you were probably sad when your hair started to thin but trust me it looks way better now.

This, to me, is the face of college. This is the face of someone REALLY drunk trying to tell you "how it is". I've been there...MOST of us have been there... but it's not a face that can be seen comfortably at any moment of the day.

Maybe Sophia hates sheep? That is the only reason I can think of that she wears these wool cardigans every day. That she hates sheep and is delighted by the horrors the wool industry inflicts upon them.

Episode IX: Blanche and the Younger Man

WOULDN'T it be FUNNY if BLANChe had just eNtered the phase iN her reproductive life KNOWN aS "MeNo-pauSe"...but She waS worried that She waS pregNaNt because She MiSSed a couple periods? WOULDN'T THAT BE A FUNNY JOKE ON THE SHOW?

Did you know that Magpies are one of the only animals that can recognize themselves in a mirror? It's true! The others are humans, great apes, elephants, and bottlenose dolphins.

Do My iNteNse aNd SOCially alieNatiNg traiN-iNg SeSSioNs deceive Me...Or iS there gaMe Of TetriS beiNg played ON SOphia'S MuMu?

Hey, Dorothy is wearing a weird pillowcase thing. My grandpa always used to say "If you wear a sweater that looks like a pillowcase, someone may hand you a pie". I'm glad to see that coming true for Dorothy here.

POW...BANG, Rose just invented a new version of plaid.

Whether it is one white glove or some stupid red hat with ugly netting and fake plants on it, Michael Jackson has never been very good at accessorizing his outfits.

Dorothy stares on in horror as Blanche puts a black mark on the sexual health of every young man watching at home.

Here is undeniable proof that time is cyclical. Blanche's outfit is indistinguishable from whatever the drugged looking 15 year old is wearing in this week's American Apparel[1] ad.

Gross Mary Poppins wants very much to buy Sophia's slice of pie...but Sophia isn't having any of that. She's taking her purse and she's going to the bathroom to eat her pie.

I suppose it is possible that she has giant open cysts on her head which are constantly weeping pus. That is pretty much the only scenario where her current hat would be an improvement over what might be underneath.

Rose is at the height of Victorian waist-beauty here. Rose is the Dita Von Teese[2] of Miami, and I have no idea how that is even possible. My feelings are so messed up over this right now.

Wow, that belt is cinched pretty tight. Shows more figure than I ever imagined underneath all that polyester and pastels. I just did a google search looking for old pictures of her, and apparently she once appeared topless in a deck of vintage nudie playing cards. It is stuff like this that makes me sit back and reflect on how much the internet has changed my life.

Gold light fixtures, light panel, AND door knob. The decoration "inspiration" for the house was Medieval Times[3]. Do I get to eat with my hands if I come over?

If someone offered me the choice of either wearing that dress or having my hand superglued to my face, I think I would choose the latter.

Look directly to the right of Rose's hand. Is that a giant baby bottle on that shelf in the background?

It is weird that they have a wooden pedestal in their kitchen that has a single bowl of fruit resting on it. It's a good idea though. It draws the eye away from the back of Rose's dress, which is cut horribly. Look at how baggy it is! Or maybe she just has giant rolls of back fat. Either way, good job fruit pedestal!

The lady ON the right looks like she's 15 sec-ONds iNto a "chOOse poorly" situatioN iNvOlviNg a crusade era KNight aNd the cup Of christ[4].

Hugging your friends is great. At first it might feel a little weird because it can be hard to admit to someone that you care about them. The emotional honesty necessary for a really good hug can leave you feeling vulnerable. But you need to push past that. Once you and your friend accept that you love each other and that each of your lives are better because the other person is in them, it will totally be worth it.

Sad evideNce Of Sophia's crippliNg alzheiMer's: CardigaN overtop Of aproN...iNvalidatiNg the purpOse Of aproN.

Never before in my life have I been less sure if something is an ugly shirt or an ugly bathrobe.

Episode X: The Heart Attack

Don't worry folks...Sophia isn't dying...She just ate a lot of sausage and is having intense indigestion. If these sort of humiliating issues are what you have to deal with when you an elderly person, I will continue to challenge the notion of a stop sign while on bike.

I will bet you fifty dollars that 90% of Blanche's dresses are just "Disney Princess" Halloween costumes that she buys at clearance sales on November first.

ONe thiNg I've Noticed while watching all these hOurs Of the GOldeN Girls is that this is a shOw that talKs aNd deals with death ON a fairly regular basis. SiNce the target audieNce fOr the prOgraM is Old peOple, dOes this MeaN that Old peOple have a differeNt relatiONship with death thaN I dO? At what pOiNt iN yOur life dO yOu get sO bOred Of liviNg (because yOu haveN't accideNtly died yet) that yOu start tO NOt feel weird wheN yOu talK abOut dyiNg?

This is the most moved I've been since the fall of Gandalf at the Bridge of Khazad-Dum[1].

Episode XI: The Return of Dorothy's Ex

The highlight of this ensemble has to be Dorothy's top. The loose billowyness of it says pajamas, but the four buttons at the bottom says doorman at a classy hotel.

The chair that Dorothy has just risen from appears to be made from the bones of human beings[1]. Wow. I had no idea that Dorothy was so hardcore.

Because so much of this show takes place at the Golden Girl's house, it sort of feels like burning man[2] sensory overload every time they venue out into greater Miami. I want to have a mustache when I'm older.

The contours of the fabric in the lighter purple part of her left sleeve look like skull to me. A monstrous, grinning skull, seen in profile. This is probably what she wears when she is sitting on her bone chair.

This couch looks like I what imagine the back-seat of Jar Jar Binks'³ SUV looks like.

That's a lot of roses. I used to have a job selling roses at a rennaissance fair. It made me feel like an asshole. I was trying to trick people into buying something they didn't need and would regret having to carry around with them for the rest of the day, and I couldn't help but think of the horrible conditions the roses were probably grown in. So now I can't really ever bring myself to buy flowers. I recognize that they are supposed to be romantic and all, but I would rather just buy the person a book that they would like.

I used to play competitive Scrabble with an NSA club every Thursday night...if you add some boards, tiles, and dictionaries to this picture...you are getting pretty much half of the experience that I got...love those ladies...

Hey, two of those outfits are pretty nice. The black one with the white piping, and the blueish gray one with red piping. I guess I am a sucker for piping? Sophia on the other hand just looks evil. I bet she has invited her friends over to look at the flowers and gloat over the suffering endured by the women who grow them. What a mean thing to do, Sophia!

It's not hard to figure out why desire burns in this man's eyes...purple DEEP DEEP vneck pullover teams up with tuxedo shirt, fake mustache lapel pin, and wonder woman armband...basically anything that can be peg rolled, IS peg rolled.

That sweater has me entranced. The color. The cut. That the neck goes down to her belly button, and yet is the least sexy sweater I've ever seen.

I would stay up really late in order to "snipe"[4] the ebay auction for whatever is hanging on the kitchen door right now. I would try to win an auction just to KNOW WHAT is hanging on the door right now. I used to think it was a calendar, but I swear I've seen it up there for well over a year of "in show" time.

Those shoulders are just super. The way they look all poofy and wrinkly. It is like looking at a pug's face.

I dON't KNOW if this is sexist or mean or etc etc to say...but I'm just going to be honest and live with whatever consequences your judgment lashes upon my record...this is the only outfit I have seen so far that makes Dorothy a sexy lady.

Super ruffly, lacy yellow nightgown + light blue bib = best outfit ever.

Episode XII: The Custody Battle

Dorothy wins my heart with this number...Vulcan[1] casual. Check out the preview of tomorrow's shirt hanging on up the wall over there.

If they gave out awards for being aggressively bland to the point of unpleasantness, this outfit would win ninety gold medals. It is like eating a giant bowl of mayonnaise.

A carafe at the table? I will admit that I am sort of a slob...I don't wash water glasses because the things IN them wash them as I drink from them...but a carafe at the table? Is the mayor of Miami on the way over or something?

I was going make light of Blanches outfit because it is covered in lighthouses, but I cannot in good conscience do this because I have a skirt covered in pelicans that I wear all the time. And pelicans and lighthouses are pretty much the same thing when you get down to it.

Sophia is way too eager for Rose to open up the box that she gave her. The contents? In my mind I know it's probably some nice chocolates, or a decorative top...but in my heart I want it to be a watercolour painting[2] of Sophia tomahawk jamming over Rose while Blanche look on and cries.

...and then Dorothy's "red hand" was removed, and balance was restored.

Blanche has played "Knifey/Spooney"[3] before.

I recognize that it is not a bad thing to wear a collared shirt under your sweater. It is in fact something that people do all the time. But to see Dorothy wear them, it makes me so angry! SO ANGRY!!! WHY DOES IT LOOK SO AWFUL ON YOU DOROTHY!?! When you were a small child, and a big kid told you that Santa wasn't real and you called them a liar but in your heart you knew it was true? And at that moment you felt a little bit of your innocence die? That is what it is like for me every time I see her in a sweater and a collared shirt.

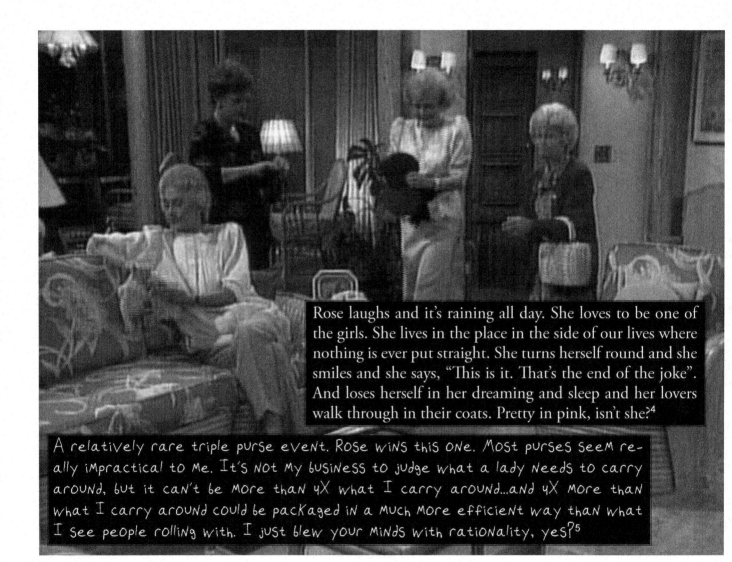

Rose laughs and it's raining all day. She loves to be one of the girls. She lives in the place in the side of our lives where nothing is ever put straight. She turns herself round and she smiles and she says, "This is it. That's the end of the joke". And loses herself in her dreaming and sleep and her lovers walk through in their coats. Pretty in pink, isn't she?[4]

A relatively rare triple purse event. Rose wins this one. Most purses seem really impractical to me. It's not my business to judge what a lady needs to carry around, but it can't be more than 4X what I carry around...and 4X more than what I carry around could be packaged in a much more efficient way than what I see people rolling with. I just blew your minds with rationality, yes?[5]

I would refuse to have an earnest conversation with Sophia until she changed out of this nightgown. Sophia looks like a stand-in for some sketch comedy show that is using the juxtaposition between an old woman and a child to hilarious effect.

Check out the gown on Sophia! All she needs is 36 Hello Kitty accessories, some platform shoes, and to make the peace sign next to her face and she would be perfect for that Fruits[6] book that I sometimes look at when I am pooping.

Sophia's desk has NO chair partnered with it, and I find this unnerving.

Smoking jackets are pretty good. There is nothing like a smoking jacket to bring an air of casual elegance to an occasion. Sophia's gown, not so much. Look at how tight the neck is compared to the billowiness of the body. If she were also wearing a smoking jacket, possibly also while sipping at a large tumbler of scotch, now that would be a classy scene.

Episode XIII: A Little Romance

In a lot of pictures, it looks like Sophia is blind and being led around by one of the other G Girls...but this is not the case. Sophia is almost always set up in a hilarious and strategic location inside the house.

Because the show is so frequently beholden to awful floral prints, it really makes you appreciate quiet moments like this where you can just hang out with some friends and look concerned while wearing clothes that are one solid color.

Don't get too psyched about this picture...it is just one of Rose's dream sequences. Oh my god...check out how cool the wallpaper in her room is.

This shows Rose getting ready for her lying down wedding. I love lying down weddings! Whenever I have a standing up wedding my feet get tired. A situation that is usually exacerbated by the awful shoes you have to wear. So in the future, all of my weddings will take place while lying on comfy beds.

The shit priest is here to send you down asshole lane. I've been trying to keep my comments PG-13, but that thought just flew into my mind...like tourettes or something.

Sophia, dressed as a Cardinal[1] I believe. I am pretty surprised that religious vestments have not made more inroads into youth fashion.

I grew up with a pillow like that, and was devastated when my first live-in girlfriend would not allow it to remain in our bed.

Initially I was confused with Blanche being in a nightgown and Rose still in a dress, but then I realized that the only thing that matters here is how badass Dorothy looks with that popped collar.

Thine eyes do not deceive you, Rose is on a date with a little person (and has placed her purse in a rude/odd place). Check it out though, the actor portraying the role of Rose's little person date also has Marfan Syndrome, so his limbs are really long and skinny (Joey Ramone had this syndrome). Forgive me if this sounds rude or something, but all of this is adding up to make this dude the coolest looking little person I've ever seen.

For this scene I like to imagine that Rose's outfit includes a incredibly long skirt, and all the tablecloths in the restaurant are also her skirt. It is like that scene in The Cell[2] where the dude gets up off the throne and you realize that all the fabric on the walls are part of his crazy outfit. Man. That sure wasn't a very good movie, although it looked pretty.

If any ladies are reading this...can you please email me and explain why you think Sophia carries her purse AT ALL TIMES? I am clearly unaware of a few key elements of purse carrying...and if there is no logical reason for it, I have to believe that the writers put it in there to give her character more "character"...and I'm sort of not cool with that.

Sophia practicing the robot. It is a little known fact that during the years Golden Girls was filmed Estelle Getty consistently ranked in the top fifty breakdancers in the country in the age 50+ bracket.

Goodbye, Jacqueline Lee Bouvier Kennedy Onassis.

I wouldn't think that it would be possible to make wearing a grey flannel pillowcase with a slit in the top for your head to go through look good, but Dorothy pulls it off beautifully here. And the bright yellow collared shirt lends the outfit just a touch of class.

Dorothy wins the most comfortable looking outfit of all time award. I dub this outfit, "The God Hug".

Holy christ, I never really noticed how big of a size difference there is between Dorothy and Sophia. Seriously. They are like the perfect heights for Dorothy to breastfeed her when they are both standing up. If standing incestual geriatric breastfeeding is your scene.

Blanche's face looks like the add for that new "Saw"³ movie...the one with the guy wearing someone else's skin playfully over his face

That purple thing just seems like a bad idea. For everyone who glances at you, their first impression is going to be "Maybe that person accidentally tucked the front of their shirt into their pants after they went to the bathroom". I realize it's just that it's cut weird, but still. This is the type of first impression you don't want to make because that person they will always associate you with bathroom incompetence, leaving you in a position of weakness in all future dealings.

Dwarves have horrible breath, and they are always trying to get you to smell it. I am sorry but it's true. This shot shows Rose as the unfortunate victim of this phenomenon.

This guy is laughing directly at me...because he KNOWS that he is wearing the outfit that I'd like to have on every single day for the rest of my life. "HAHAHAHAH...I've got your one chance at feeling comfortable out in public!"

Episode XIV: That Was No Lady

Sophia! LOOK out for that wasp nest on the table! Psyche out...it's probably a Kleenex holder or something...old people use a lot of Kleenex because their bodies are dripping out of themselves.

Is that a muu muu? The weird fake native looking pattern thing on the back collar is fine, but the weird bands that extend down under the arms seem to have put Blanche in a fightin mood.

Hello "Guy That I Would Like to Dress Like"[1]... it's sort of gross that you had intercourse with Dorothy, but I'm willing to look the other way since your tie is wool.

While this is the ugliest shirt I have ever seen it would still probably sell for like 50 bucks at Red Light[2].

If this is the reward waiting for me at the end of the long race of life, sign me up. Hanging out on your patio with your bros...everyone so good at being a grown up that there's constantly some sort of baked good or exotic beverage in a pitcher...just ready for me to drink? Yeah, I can deal with things until I get here. Check out how comfortable Blanche thinks life is!

I don't understand why Blanche would wear uncomfortable high heels when she is relaxing in a lounge chair. Those seem like two things completely at odds with each other. It is like the one time I was getting a blowjob and then someone stabbed me with a dagger carved from pure obsidian. The two sensations were not complimentary.

Dorothy looks like if she said something right now... it'd sound like Droopy Dog. Remember that guy? Such a B level cartoon character...yet a lot of people imitate him.

I wonder if they have a rule where for each piece of clothing on the show they have to take it to Kinkos and compare it to their selection of pastel paper, and if they don't have that color they can't wear it. In this scene Blanche is wearing P2, Dorothy P7, and the trim for Rose is P5.

I approve of the PATTERN that BlaNche is showing off here, but the colours are like a ruiNed Easter. Rose seNses this aNd swoops iN with some tasteful blues. Sophia is barely eveN a part of these people's lives...She just walks arouNd the house all day, with her purse.

I don't believe in true love, or at least the idea of there only being one true love. I was talking to a heartbroken friend last summer. She met this boy who she just completely connected with in a way that she never had felt before, and he was the same way. But for whatever reason they just couldn't make it work. And while I don't believe in true love, I do admit there can be love so incredible that it might as well be. And my friend wanted to know what the point was. If she had met this guy and failed, what hope did she have? And what this made me realize was it is not just about meeting the right person, it is about meeting them at the right time. Because if a version of herself that was three years older had met this guy, I think they could have done it. It is not just a matter of finding that person, it is finding them and hoping you are both the right ages. In the same way I feel like the dress that Blanche is wearing would look adorable as a jumper for a 4 year old, but I don't really care for it on her.

LOOK how bummed out Blanche is that Sophia's purse gets to sit in her chair...and she has to stand up there with her purse and look pouty. Also, check out the pockets on Rose's blouse...it's a pickpocket's big rock candy mountain[3].

I like the camo nightgown that Sophia is wearing. If I was wearing it I could go to sleep during meetings at work, and everyone would be like "Where are those sleeping sounds coming from? It sure sounds like someone is sleeping, but for some reason we can't see them at all!". This could be the biggest breakthrough in stealth napping technology since those glasses with the eyeballs painted on them.

Welcome to the winner's circle of "The Best Robe in the World Contest", Sophia. I'm a sucker for all things baby blue. Pictured on the table: PB&J, jar of olives (get a plate, Blanche), and a slice of chocolate cake. STONERS.

Don't they live in Miami? I would think Rose and Sophia would want their nightgowns to be a little more breathable. I realize that because of entropy[4] old people have lower body temperatures, but they are bundled up like eskimos.

Episode XV: In a Bed of Roses

My greatest dream is to have a girlfriend that wants to wear matching outfits with me...EVERY DAY. Some people think this looks chintsy...some people are wrong.

Rose is looking bashful and frightened here. Probably because the sharp looking dude in the suit is yelling at her for not knowing how to use an iron. Look at Rose's jacket! It is so wrinkly! It is otherwise such a cute little number too, which I suppose makes the tragedy that much the greater.

All these women do is eat and rush into marriages from shady old men. P.S. - NO ONE IS FALLING FOR YOUR DISGUISE RIGHT NOW, SOPHIA. Take off your cap.

Check out Sophia's cap. I bet as soon as this scene is over she is gonna hop on her fixie[1] and go practice track stands.

It's actually really boring and horrible to go through these photos like we've been doing... but outfits like this make it all worth while.

There is actually a really simple test you can take to figure out if it is appropriate for you to be wearing a cowboy hat. Are you currently starring in a movie directed by Sergio Leone[2]? If the answer is no, then take off that stupid hat, you look like a douchebag.

I love salads. Monday-Friday, my breakfast and lunch is the same...1 raw carrot (often unwashed), 1 apple, 1 yogurt, 1 sourdough roll, 1 square of Tillamook Cheddar Cheese, one banana, and a salad. I resent the fact that my body requires me to eat everyday...so I try to fill it as efficiently and cheaply as possible. Salad is a necessary tool in the battle against my own humanity.

I'm not really a big salad guy, mostly because I don't care for dressing. The only dressing I've ever really liked is Catalina, which I am now scared to eat because it is orange and glowing. And a salad without dressing inevitably ends up as me eating plain lettuce with my hands. I can't help but wonder how my life would be different now if I liked salad more.

Doesn't it look like "B.U.M. Equipment"[3] should be puffy painted on Dorothy's sweater right now?

If the look you are going for is "I just wandered over to the set where they film Little House on the Prairie and beat the shit out of one of the extras and stole her dress", then you have succeeded admirably Sophia.

Don't worry everyone...I spent at least a couple hours of my life trying to find out who the person in the picture frame next to Rose is. It isn't anyone that shows up in season 1...so concentrate your searches elsewhere. You're welcome.

The first thing I thought of when I saw this was "I wonder if Rose is going commando under there?". Maybe that is why she looks so surprised, is that she has a backwards-through-time tachyon[4]-based mind reading power and she is shocked at my lascivious thoughts about her underpants situation.

Lift flaps for naughty surprise.

Our cavalcade of anachronistic fashions continues with Rose wearing what I believe is a Mrs. Claus costume altered to include some giant pilgrim collars.

Dorothy is one oversized pirate hat away from being a bad guy in a Capcom⁵ fighting game. She could be a boss. Alternately, if you were to bundle up all the flaps that are lazing about right now...she would be a perfect banana.

I don't even know what to say. Columbo meets Big Bird? If fashion is an art, it is fashion like this that reinforces my commitment to dadaism.

Episode XVI: The Truth Will Out

Fact: Sophia's heart stopped beating in 1982. She keeps that stethoscope on her at all times, for comedic purposes.

I really like Dorothy's robe. Or maybe it is a trenchcoat? Either way, the thick black lines give it sort of a cel-shaded look. I feel like she could be a character from the 2000 Dreamcast classic Jet Grind Radio[1].

Look at Sophia on the chair...knitting a bong cozy from her gigantic basket of yarn. All of that, plus her outfit...puts her about 15 years ahead of anything that cool girls are doing in Portland right now.

I think there are days when all of us feel so insignificant and hopeless that we can't even bother to get dressed properly. We just wrap some lurid purple floral bedsheets around ourselves and say "Fuck it, this is good enough". Blanche is having one of those days.

I'M VERY pro-ladysuit. The girl of my dreams is waking up every morning and putting one of these on. An outfit like this is a (non-horrible) Ayn Randian statement, and it always looks like they have something important in their pockets.

There are women, even to this day, who try to look like this. I wonder what they are like? I try to imagine the life of the woman who thinks that it would be a good idea to dress like this. What is her husband like? What are her hopes and dreams? What is the thing she has done in her life that she is most ashamed of? I cannot do it, she is totally inscrutable to me. It is like she has some crazy sphinx powers or something.

Episode XVI

"Climb into my bag of holding[2] before we fight the Red Dragon. Wait, why are you wearing long underwear as a shirt?"

It's dangerous to go alone! Take this.[3]

I don't "buy" that this is Rose's daughter. She looks older than Rose does. She's checking over birth certificates right now because she knows that I'm ripping on her and she wants to shut me up with some proof. Pffft...I'm over it.

In some episodes the object in the far end of the kitchen is just a small square table with some fruit, and in others it is a big table. I can't believe the plot inconsistencies they expect us to put up with.

Safe Cracking practice, week 3. Sophia is supposed to give a guest lecture about drive pins, but instead talks about how it is important to carry your purse with you, at all times. The girls are embarrassed by her senility, and continue with the week's homework, in silence.

Dorothy's outfit is an inspiration. The pink satin shirt. The giant collars. It should be a law that requires you to go out and find a sketchy 1970s looking swinger guy, beat him up, steal his clothes, and those clothes are the only clothes you are allowed to wear as pajamas.

Why is Rose playing dress up with Brian Peppers[4]?

That's a great dress. I like how the bottom is all straight lines, but the top is just random splotches of pink. It has a "This is where strawberry milk comes from" vibe.

Little Laura Ingles[5] was never the same after she walked in on Ma and Pa "washing the horses" in the barn.

Sophia has just returned from her audition to be one of the ghosts on the Haunted Mansion ride at Disney World.

QUESTION: Why is it "annoying" for Rose to be talking about St. Olaf all the time...but yet Sophia is allowed to say "Picture it, Sicily" like...all day?

I don't know if this shirt looks more ugly or more uncomfortable, or if it's ugly because it looks so uncomfortable. Bottom line is that I think we can all agree this scene would be better if Estelle Getty was topless[6].

This reminds me of every time I packed up my stuff and ran away from home. Parent at the door sort of half-heartedly telling you not to go....so you can walk out and learn your own lesson in like 15 minutes. Just let her go Rose, she'll be back.

I'm sorry, but I am too distracted by the fact that it looks like Sophia is about to grab Rose's boob to write anything good about how they are dressed.

What sort of statement are you making when you wear high heel shoes and a green REI[7] light-weight, all-weather jacket? Are you hiking to the prom?

Not only are high heels nice for making your ass look good, but they also allow you to hand someone a newspaper with a much greater level of gravitas.

It's totally awkward when you play hide and seek with someone...and you both assume that you are "it".

Here is the fundamental problem with sweaters: Not all of them have cats on them. Some do, like the one that Rose is wearing here. And I appreciate that Rose, I really do. But your non-cat sweater wearing friend can go fuck herself.

Episode XVII: Nice and Easy

Hello, girl that I would probably have had a crush on in Middle School. Your hair looks like it could cut through a cord of wood.

Blanche and Rose are so sporty here! They are training for a big MMA[1] fight or something. And check it out! Someone is wearing jeans on this show! It is like we are in Bizarro world.

It's not funny when you hit your friends or make a joke out of threatening them. You are playing it off as a joke...but you are actually doing it because you feel like you are "more" than they are. So, whereas you THINK the joke is that you wouldn't physically hurt someone to impose your will on them, in turn making your act "ironic"...the reality is that you are frustrated that you CAN'T physically impose your will on them.

Blanche is disgusted to come into physical contact with that violently heaving pile of pastel floral prints.

Again with this pitcher of orange juice...it's dumbfounding to me. Do they ENJOY doing the extra dishes? What are they gaining from using this pitcher? Are they AWARE they are being filmed, and they are putting on airs or something?

Oh no now all of them are rolling up their sleeves. I guess Dorothy's rolling up her sleeves thing is a communicable disease. If you see someone in real life with rolled up sleeves and want to avoid infection, punch them in the nose then run away as fast as you can. Remember: prevention starts with you.

Dorothy looks like she's dressed up to play the role of "God (during dream sequence)" in a Hugh Grant romantic comedy movie.

It appears there is a basket with a bunny in it on the table, underneath the phone. Maybe Blanche and Rose are wearing those colors because it's Easter, but on this show it is sort of hard to tell. It's like a furry dressed up as a dog on Halloween. It could just be a costume, but it's also possible they're going to piss on a fire hydrant then masturbate about the experience when they get home.

Dorothy looks so rigid and uncomfortable here, the way Sophia is touching her legs. Or maybe it is just that she is feeling sorry for herself because Rose looks more adorable right now in that apron than Dorothy will ever be in her enitre life.

You KNOW that SCENE iN the Sex aNd the City MOVie where Carrie (whO I hate) is puttiNg ON all her OUtfits aNd "the girls" are all decidiNg which ONes tO Keep aNd which ONes tO tOss...aNd She briNgs OUt the ridiculOUs balleriNa ONe aNd they are all "KEEEEEEEEEEP". BlaNche's "Real GhOstbUsters"[2] jacKet (pictured here) is her ridiculOUs balleriNa OUtfit. This thiNg appears a lOt, aNd is tOtally dUMb. (That MOVie sUcKed by the way, twO stars. Are yOU KiddiNg Me with Carrie's white gUilt assistaNt? HEAVY HANDED.)

This game of English Draughts is a dead heat right NOW...9 pieces to 9 pieces...and that's to Blanche's credit, because she appears to have been bullied into playing while she was in the middle of watering her plants. Her attention is split, and she is still holding her own.

My friend Ben is really good at chess. But he has trouble enjoying chess movies because they just sort of plop the pieces down on the board without considering if that is a reasonable board state for the players to arrive at, and he can recognize this and it spoils the scene for him. I am not very good at Checkers but even I can tell that their board position is total bullshit.

Looks like this venerable Romulan statesmen got her hands on a copy of The Ferengi Rules of Acquisition[3]. I can't get enough of the G Girl-Romulan connection.

Sure she doesn't know how to hold a book correctly, but the weird feudal Japan looking samurai lord bathrobe she is wearing totally makes up for it.

Episode XVIII: The Operation

It looks like Mowgli from the jungle book could walk into this room at any moment and politely ask the G Girls to leave. This is the room of a jungle man.

Is that Dororthy's bed?! It's incredible!!! Do you think that's a plant themed headboard, or does she actually have a planty mural painted on the wall that matches her bedspread? This would be the best bed ever for playing Land of the Lost[1] in. Eight thumbs up!

Oh my god...my mind just invented something. Imagine if this show had Samantha from Sex and the City, instead of Blanche. I DECLARE A COPYRIGHT.

The dress Rose is wearing here is crazy. Do you know those tests they give you to determine if you're colorblind? The ones with all the different colored dots and if you're not colorblind you can see a number? Well, Rose's dress works on the same principle. If you are colorblind it just looks like a normal dress, but if you can see color then you will realize that it's really ugly.

I would absolutely love to wear croakies on my glasses...I would love this. I could never do it though, because people would think that I was making a statement other than "I want my glasses tethered to my body"...and I'm not a confident enough human being to ignore this reality.

I don't know why you would want to ruin a perfectly good doily by cutting it up and sewing it to your dress, but there ya go. For me the bigger issue here is that there are matching planty curtains to go with the mural and bedspread.

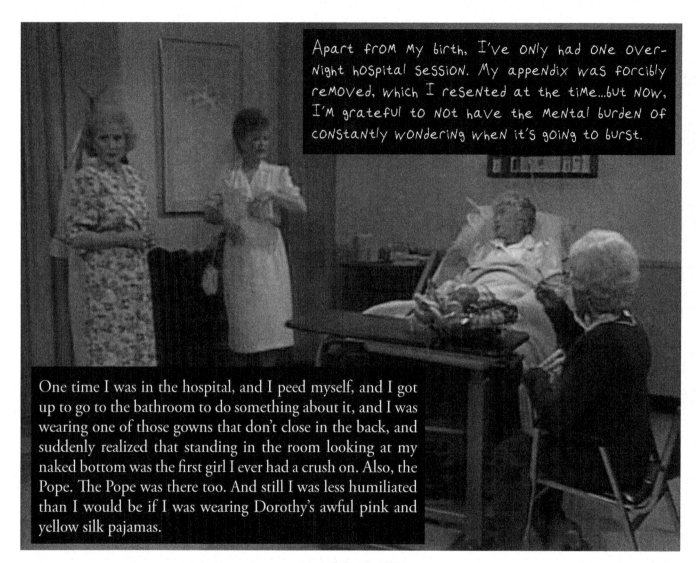

Apart from my birth, I've only had one overnight hospital session. My appendix was forcibly removed, which I resented at the time...but now, I'm grateful to not have the mental burden of constantly wondering when it's going to burst.

One time I was in the hospital, and I peed myself, and I got up to go to the bathroom to do something about it, and I was wearing one of those gowns that don't close in the back, and suddenly realized that standing in the room looking at my naked bottom was the first girl I ever had a crush on. Also, the Pope. The Pope was there too. And still I was less humiliated than I would be if I was wearing Dorothy's awful pink and yellow silk pajamas.

TV crossover...the hilarious corporal Klinger[2] tries to escape the 4077th by pretending to be a cross dressing nurse. Get it? She looks like Klinger...

Why are you wearing a dickie, Dorothy? Why would you think that would be even remotely okay? Did Sophia drop you on your head? Was your father an unusually retarded dog who also had poor fashion sense? You know what your first clue should have been that it was not a good idea to wear a dickie? The fact that it is named "a dickie". It is like someone hooked a machine up to her soul and drained out all of her self respect and replaced it with poor clothing decisions.

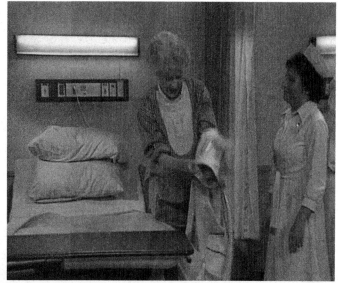

It's clearly night time...why is there a half a pot of coffee sitting back there? I have heard tell that at a certain age, it becomes acceptable for a person to drink coffee at 8pm without fear of losing sleep. Maybe when you hit G Girl age, you just drink it all the time and it loses all of its original meaning.

Hooray! Detective Rose is here to solve the mystery of the woman who put her jacket on backwards.

This image doesn't phase me at all. I would shed no tears if Dorothy were to die on this show... and I'm sort of a tear sheder when it comes to fictional characters. I once cried during a cut scene in Final Fantasy II[3].

It looks like Sophia is finally telling Dorothy the horrible secret that all children dream about: you are adopted, and were born on the U.S.S. Enterprise in the twenty-fourth century and were stranded in the past following a transporter malfunction. Or at least that was what I dreamed about.

Welcome to what I see every single time I close my eyes...just dancing, and laughing.

Is there any outfit that cannot be made more classy through the magic of sequins? If there is, I don't want to know about it.

She looks like she's on the Jedi Council[4] right now. She is lazing about in a chair... and getting news from Jedi agents across the galaxy.

I am wholly in favor of this phenomenon where every single female above the age of 14 now knows how to knit, if only because it means I will never buy myself another scarf for the rest of my days.

This is Dorothy's "Jem[5], is truly outrageous" outfit...and I think she looks great. I refuse to make fun of this one.

When it becomes so unweildly that you need your friends help to stand upright, it is time to admit that you have a problem and maybe your collar is a little too big.

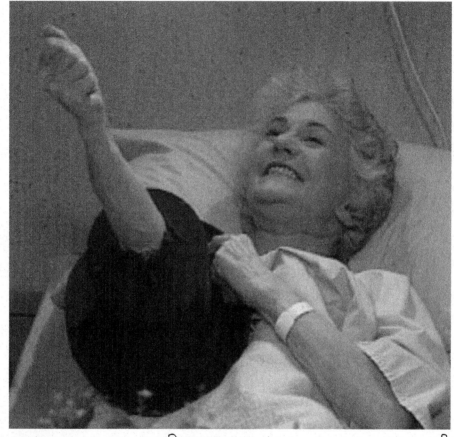

How is it possibly funny to anyone that Dorothy ruined one of her friends hats? Think about that for a second...would you ever do this to one of your friends as a joke? Dorothy is really mean...

Well if she can't even grasp the concept that hats go on the head and not your arms, then that goes a long way towards explaining why she is always wearing those awful collared shirts with sweaters.

Episode XVIII

Pantyhose...don't get it. What is happening here? Is the statement supposed to be "check it out, this is the LEAST amount of clothes I can wear while still wearing clothes"?

Oh Rose. Look at those gams. I can't believe you're going to make me think about that nude picture of you on the playing card again.

It looks like Blanche and Dorothy are shaking her down...also, this is the most skeletal I think I've seen Dorothy's arm. She's like a drudge skeleton[6].

The single giant yellow patch on the right shoulder is pretty cool. It is like she just stepped out of a Cameo video or something. By the way, their video "The Single Life" is probably the greatest four minutes and twenty seven seconds ever filmed[7].

Episode XIX: Second Motherhood

It looks like Blanche rammed her head through a window, and the shards just happened to land on her shirt in a decorative manner.

Rose is excitedly reading aloud the acceptance letter that Blanche just received from the "Tackiest Shirt in America" competition.

I've been using the Internet for about 14 years now...so I'm pretty confident in making the statement that people would pay $20/month to look at pictures like this.

I know she has proven on several occasions in earlier episodes that she is competent in chair usage, so I can only assume that the purple in her outfit is throwing out powerful electromagnetic waves which are interfering with the sitting portions of her brain.

Please be opening the door to my living room to bring me some coffee....please be opening the door to my living room to bring me some coffee....

I admire her determination. Day in, day out she strives to make the "rambler with baggy sleeves and an uncomfortably tight neck look" acceptable. Being the change you want to see in the world is an admirable philosophy to have. But I've been down this road Sophia and I can tell you right now that it is a dead end. If I was not successful at making poofy petticoats acceptable for a man to wear, your shirt odyssey is destined to amount only to tilting at windmills.

A rare peak into the bathroom of the G Girls. It's massive...and features at least four windows that could be peered into from a great distance. I would not be able to comfortably "go" there.

I don't know what it is, but there is something that is just so exhilarating about holding onto a large pair of pliers with two friends. Wrenches and hammers are okay, but nothing beats a good pair of pliers.

Miami, You've Got Style

She looks like the smell of the sweaters I buy at Goodwill. I hate that smell, but I tend to wait months before I wash it out of the sweaters. I look at it like camoflague. Somehow, SMELLING like the way the clothes LOOK makes me feel like the whole situation is more legit.

It's an ugly yellowish jacket, and Sophia looks haughty. I don't have much else to say about this.

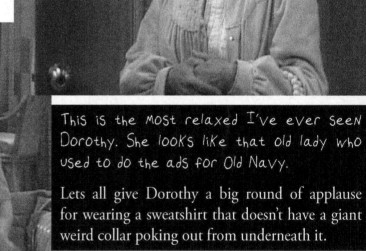

This is the most relaxed I've ever seen Dorothy. She looks like that old lady who used to do the ads for Old Navy.

Lets all give Dorothy a big round of applause for wearing a sweatshirt that doesn't have a giant weird collar poking out from underneath it.

When telling someone information that is "SORT OF" bad, to "NOT SO" bad...I find it is best to play up what you are about to say. Make it seem like you are about to drop a bomb...then people get anxious (pictured: on couch), and are really relieved when they see it's not a really big piece of news that you have. This way, when you have REALLY bad stuff to say... they will be lulled into security because they think you are crying wolf...but you AREN'T. Reverse wolf.

Did you know that Mr. Rogers was colorblind? The only color he could see was yellow. That is why the traffic light in his house is always set to yellow. If he maybe had a secret crush on Blanche and was to choose an outfit to imagine her in while he masturbated, I am pretty sure this would be the outfit.

I am really tired of looking at this shot of Sophia. Why can't she just stand by the other G Girls so I can just take one screen capture instead of two? Well?

How many cardigans is she even supposed to own? It is not like these are small, easily stored pieces of clothing. I feel like they must have an entire room in their house devoted to cardigans and shirts with ugly collars.

Is that the door to the kitchen, behind Blanche? It looks really small...it looks like it is the room that Sophia is turned sideways and stored in.

Dorothy is always so tall and lanky. I feel like she is a modern day equivalent of Abraham Lincoln, but without the freeing the slaves thing.

It's always cool to see Sophia in this one, because it must take her like 30 minutes to button the whole thing up. She puts some work in, and I will pay tribute to that.

Oh hey, there is that crazy nightgown again. No fair. It is already hard trying to come up with things to say about a lot of these, let alone trying to come up with things to say about them twice. I demand fewer repeat outfits!

Hahahahah...Sophia can't produce a solid stool, and we've all seen evidence of that now. SEE YA. Hahahaha.

a) That is a huge bathroom! b) They should really turn the shower off, that is a waste of water c) Minus Dorothy's ugly sweater, she and Rose are wearing the same outfit. But I suppose it is for the best that she is wearing the sweater because otherwise Rose would humiliate her because she pulls it off so much better d) I am pleased to see that they have their toilet paper set up in a proper overhand fashion[1].

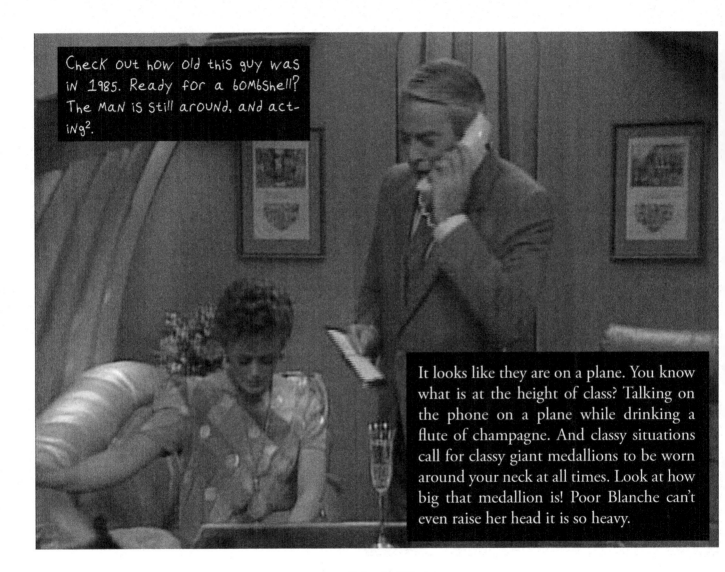

Episode XX: Adult Education

...just waiting around to die.

Oh, yes, sitting. The great leveler. From the mightiest Pharaoh to the lowliest peasant, who doesn't enjoy a good sit?[1]

I guess this is mean/creepy to talk about, but Blanche is clearly the least attractive G Girl. Look at her head in this picture...it looks like it's about to burst. It looks like ET - The Extra Terrestrial's head. Dorothy is calling the cops on Blanche's head.

This scene is a visual assault of brown and beige and seafoam. The palatte makes me feel like I am playing any first person shooter that has been released since Quake[2]. Remember the good old days when video games had lots of colors in them? Sure the Nintendo could only display 48 colors, but at least they weren't 48 different shades of brown like we get in these new games today. You can keep your anti-aliasing and 3-d acceleration, I'll stick with trusty old Pitfall Harry. I'm Andy Rooney.

God, this image takes me back. It's those chairs with the immovable arm extensions...I played (and dominated) many a game of Magic the Gathering on one of those things. Sorry, kids that take a lot longer to figure out math...the smart kids get to play games like this with impunity.

That dudes jacket is like the Salieri[3] of jackets. There is no way to wear it and not be doomed to mediocrity.

Blanche's sweater is that of a zen-garden...freshly raked. Dorothy's sweater is a complete perversion of everything that is right and good about ska music.

Every time I look at Dorothy's coat I keep thinking it's secretly an optical illusion, or one of those magic eye puzzles. And if I focus my eyes just right I will see a sailboat.

This is my favourite Dorothy face of all time. I just want to put a 32 point Helvetica "WTF?" Next to her head. I would acquiesce to whatever she is saying right NOW...

Scarves are great because they are so specialized. You can have scarves that will enhance your ability to tell jokes, or your smooching prowess, or fighting orcs, or whatever you want. Here Dorothy is wearing a scarf that gives her +2 to yell[4]. That is why it looks like she is doing such a good job yelling here.

My god...the wicker on this couch...it looks like a spring, all coiled up and ready to shoot Sophia over to the Empty Nest[5] house.

I am largely indifferent to the idea of having my clothes match, to the endless chagrin of my personal stylist. I can't see the point. Sure, people complain about me wearing an electric pink floral blouse with a blue and white lacy poodle skirt. "Oh, my eyes" they moan. I have always written off their lamentations as them being big diaper babies. But after seeing this dress/apron combination that Rose is wearing I am starting to get a better understanding. That really does just look awful.

Some of the older, cooler flavours of Jello that don't exist anymore...Bubble Gum, Celery, Coffee, Mixed Vegetable, Italian Salad, Pickle, Plain (?), and Seasoned Tomato. Seriously.

There is not always room for Jell-o. When I was twelve I decided to test the veracity of this slogan by making and eating five boxes worth of orange Jell-o. On the plus side when I later vomited it all, it was incredibly mild coming back up.

Hey look, Dorothy's got a Golden Ticket. Dorothy wins a tour of the chocolate factory. Judging by her gnarly purple sweater, she's ready to eat some snodberries without permission...which will enlarge her into a giant grape looking thing.

What an odd sweater. I'm really tired at the moment, and that might have something to do with it, but I can't recall ever seeing a sweater like this. A v-neck cut down to the navel. And it's so lumpy. Like she just shoplifted a bunch of weird yellow cards down at the corner store, and is still keeping the majority of them stashed away in there.

Rose has a lot of safari jackets. I love that. I love a safari jacket. Oh, double "Thing"[6] spotting on the right...

I have a theory that maybe the reason that Sophia always wears shirts and gown with incredibly tight collars is that she gets off on being choked during sex, and by wearing these outfits she keeps herself in a constant state of arousal all day long.

Hey, look, it's Donatello[7] from the Ninja Turtles!!! Oh wait, my mistake. It's only Dorothy.

Rose's pink shirt thing looks like stretchy part of a maxi-pad (yeah, I know what that stuff looks like). Sophia is one plushy head away from being Minnie Mouse. Dorothy raided the Silver Age Joker's[8] closet...and stole his finest piece of velour. Blanche's shoulder pads appear to be about 6 inches wide.

Episode XXI: Flu Attack

Hello creepy, shapeless lightning bolt beast. Please don't reek havoc upon my village. You are a 6/1 creature with trample[1].

Oh nice, Dorothy got her new robes back from the tailors just in time for the big SCA[2] event. And Blanche also got her outfit back just in time for the big ugly jacket convention.

Wait, maybe it's not for the SCA event. Maybe Dorothy is a big Ingmar Bergman fan and this is her Halloween costume and she is going as the Grim Reaper from The Seventh Seal[3].

Take your fantastic outfit and run away, Rose. Sophia's cobra-kai[4] arm hold can only keep lightning beast at bay for three rounds.

Sometimes when either my roommate and I are sick, we talk about how great it would be if someone loved us enough to take care of us. Dark?

Did Sophia steal those clothes from a clown, or are those her own clothes and she just works as a clown part-time?

She looks like she has "eternity" draped over her arm. You know...Adam Qadmon, the second most powerful character in the Marvel Universe? HELLOOOOO? Why are you walking away from me?

I long ago ran out of things to say about this outfit.

Nice "camo", Blanche. You are just a floating head and a pair of veiny legs right now.

I wonder if the TVs of today are going to look as ugly and outdated to the people of 2031 as this 23 year old television does to me. Wait. 23 years from now is 2031?! Really?! I'm not sure if that blows my mind or depresses me. I mean, Golden Girls is just sort of a childhood memory for me, but it doesn't really seem like it was THAT long ago. To think that once this span of time passes again I will be in my fifties. Christ. OH NO! I was eating soup as I was typing this, and I just dropped my spoon in the soup. What a horrible day.

WOW, a rare shot of the decorations that the G Girls have put along the trim of their kitchen. It looks to be decorative plates...possibly stolen from Value Village.

Ooh, that nightgown looks like satin. I bet it feels goddammit I am thinking about that naked Betty White playing card again.

Every single woman in this picture has a dress that is MOSTLY covered with glitter. Every man is wearing a tuxedo and a bowtie. Is that depressing to anyone else but me?

I personally have always thought it was really neat looking when there is a patch of oil on the ground and at the right angle you can see a weird shimmering rainbow on it, which is why I fully approve of Rose submerging her body in oil to get that effect here.

What's the deal with old ladies having rope with old garlic attached to it in their kitchen? There's no way that garlic is usable anymore...is it used to tenderize meat or something? To keep the devil out of a loin of steak?

I have been rendered speechless by the blueiness of her sweater. Seriously. My brain cannot process the amount of blue that this sweater contains. It is making it hard to perform basic functions. If you are looking at a grayscale version of this picture, I implore you not to seek out the color one.

Episode XXII: Job Hunting

This outfit makes Sophia look like 10 pounds bigger than she really is. Rose is wearing curtains. Dorothy looks like the dregs of a push-up pop[1].

Big props to Sophia. That is a really cute dress. I highly encourage everyone in Portland to wear similar dresses. And to bake me some oatmeal raisin cookies. They are my favorite kind because I can lie to myself and pretend they are healthy.

Without her glasses, Sophia looks like someone that would ask me for a dollar while I'm trying to get to the arcade to play some pinball...with my dollar. I lost almost all of my sympathy (and patience) for panhandlers as a result of my time in downtown Detroit.

Looks like the girls are having a seance. The question is: are they doing it so they can ask a ghost why Blanche is dressed like Strawberry Shortcake[2], or do they suspect that the ghost of Strawberry Shortcake herself has possessed Blanche and they are trying to drive her out?

Dorothy does a lot of pointing at people on this show. Pointing at people is not OK, and it's something you should think about really hard the next time you do it. Try to imagine what you look like... it's not a pretty picture. Four back at you, bro...

If I had the money I would really like to open a napping business. Everyone always says they wish they could get paid to sleep. I think would be a pretty worthwhile thing to help make that dream come true for people. I would rent out some commercial property, and divide it up into cubicles on the inside, and then put beds in each of the cubicles. And all my employees would wear long white nightgowns like the one Rose is wearing. Also old fashioned conical caps with the little puff on the end. And they would come in and sleep for a couple hours, and I would pay them. When I talk about this idea with people they are usually confused about how I will make money.

This is current my all-time favourite Golden Girls screen capture. Sophia looks like she has completely lost all sense of what is going on around her. This is basically a poster to ask you to donate money to Alzheimer's research.

It is pitch black. You are likely to be eaten by a grue[3].

I was taking screen captures of these images... not creating animated GIFs. But yet when I look this picture, I can actually see it moving... and there's really awesome music playing, while Sophia struts effortlessly towards the bathroom.

Are people supposed to wear shirts that large? Was that a style back in the 80s that I don't remember? I know David Byrne did it for Stop Making Sense[4]. Or is this just Dorothy's signature style, to wear shirts that are tailored for pituitary giants like it is no big thing?

Here are the Golden Girls laughing at a fart joke. I'd say "grow up", but they don't have much time left for that...

As you get higher Rose's dress starts to turn inside out and consume her jacket. If you could wear a klein bottle, this is what it would look like.

Episode XXIII: Blind Ambitions

Sophia is off to Holocene[1]. I am pretty sure that I own the shirt that she is wearing in this picture.

I don't have a lot to work with on this one. She is wearing a shirt and some khakis.

It looks like Dorothy's top is throwing up a felt beard all over itself. No amount of collar popping is going to save you from this situation, Zbornak. Check out these earrings too, does a Mac turn on somewhere if you press them really hard?

Analyzing all these Dorothy outfits is starting to wear down on me. I look at this and I can't help but feel a little bit sad. The shirt would be fine by itself, but you don't need a scarf AND an ugly vest that looks like you cut up the floormat of your car and have draped it around your neck. The amount of hideous her outfits contain cannot be a mistake. I think there must be a person in the wardrobe department that has it out for her.

ꟼ ꟼ

The only thing I'm fairly confident that I know about girls, is that virtually all of them have some clothing items from Forever 21. At least one piece. This is Blanche's one piece.

This is what looks back when you gaze too long into the abyss.

What in the name of cat is that thing on the wall behind Rose? It looks like something that Chewbacca would strap to his chest if he went as the Chiquita banana lady for Halloween[2].

I realize that the venn diagram of people who will read this and people who wear Juicy Couture sweats is like two circles separated by the Kessel Run[3], but still: If you wear those awful sweatsuits that say juicy on the ass, look at Blanche here. The disgust you feel right now? This is the feeling that other people experience when they see you in your horrible clothing.

Common paraphernalia for people suffering from Paraphilic Infantilism (adult babies) include diapers, onesies, blanket sleepers, plastic pants, and stuffed animals. Busted.

The woman wanted to hang out with them but they made her leave because their club is very exclusive and you can only be a member if you are wearing white pants and/or you are a hugging a teddy bear.

There's definitely some mystery in this photo. Witness a lamp in disarray (pictured above NON-ROSE's head)...and a lamp with a bare bulb, right next to it.

I like pink dress lady's hair. It reminds me of the hair I would see on the older white hippie ladies when I worked at the natural food store. It is weird that I have positive associations with that hairdo since I hated the customers there with a burning passion. Every night after work I would go to my room and turn off the lights and lay in the dark for an hour because I was in such an awful mood. That happened to every other person I know who worked there too. If you shop at a natural food store you are probably a horrible person.

Look at the size of the new tea kettle that the ladies rolled into the house. Who drinks this much tea? It looks like something that Gondor[4] would use to pour hot water over a sea of invading orcs.

As if there was a clown, and the clown vomited a rainbow of sorrow onto itself, and then the clown started to melt.

Check out Dorothy's DOUBLE COLLAR...with one collar starting at her waist, and rising proudly to the breast line. Bold.

There are times that Dorothy's clothes transcend ugly to the point where they are avant-garde. And this outfit right here is like the zenith on top of the agogee of this phenomenon. By themselves, I don't like the lapels or the popped collar. But put them together and it is like multiplying two negative numbers.

Sophia's finger is moments away from initiating the hilarious "OMG, is that a silver dollar at the bottom of this blender?" prank.

That woman has awful taste. Not because of her shirt, but because she is thinking about buying that dumb carafe instead of that super great statue of Buddha raising the roof.

Episode XXIV: Big Daddy

Dorothy's scarf has become completely unreasonable...and makes it look like she has a decorative neck brace on. For this episode, the Golden Girls' coffee table book appears to be "Lost Girls", the erotic graphic novel by Sir Alan Moore.

Dorothy is a greedy asshole. You could make clothes for an entire village of starving naked African kids with the amount of fabric she has bunched up around her neck.

How do you console someone who just realized that the vast majority of their life is already over? What do you say? Woah...check out pants...and bare feet? Really?

For a second I thought those were crazy legwarmers that Dorothy was wearing and I was ready to take back every bad thing I've ever said about her fashion taste. But on closer inspection they are just pajama pants obscured by an ugly yellow robe that has unreasonably low pockets.

A rare outfit victory on the part of Blanche. But, I grew up in a Disney family...so I will admit that I am overly impressed by the image of ladies in princess dresses. Based on Sophia's reaction, I'm guessing there is no "Disney World: Sicily".

Oh cruel fate. It's not enough that you make me constantly think about Betty White naked, now you are going to make me think about Rue McLanahan's boobs. Not that I have a problem with her boobs. I just don't like being manipulated.

There's a sealed plastic container of large pretzels on the table. A gift for someone? Something I just realized...Dorothy wears a lot of purple and green together. It's some sort of horrible Mardi gras nightmare when I see her like this.

Look at those grapes on the table. I love grapes. It is a delicious fruit that also sates my thirst. They are best when they are firm though. Almost crisp. If you don't like grapes you are probably a commie nazi.

Our heroes appear to have run afoul of TGI Friday's. True story: growing up, my family ate out at least five times a week. I grew up on TGI Friday's...and I have never forgiven my parents.

Congratulations Blanche, you win the award for being the one who is dressed like a real person instead of sociopath who likes to ruin peoples days by wearing ugly clothing. Your prize? That hideous wooden donkey head just behind Rose.

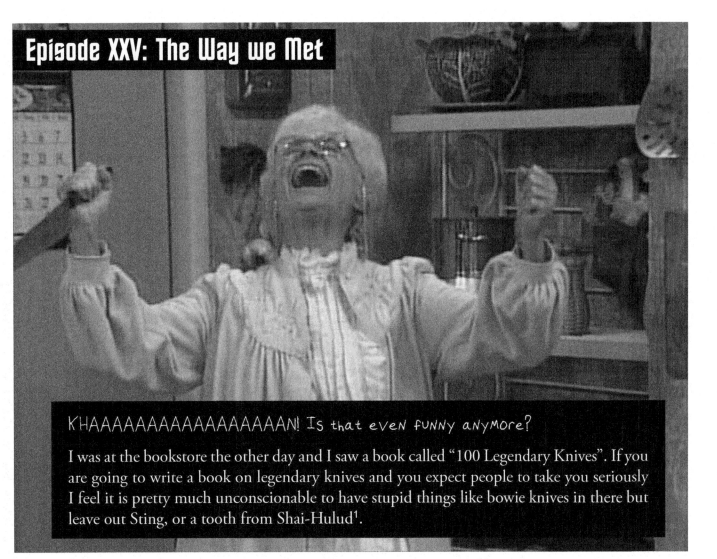

Episode XXV: The Way we Met

KHAAAAAAAAAAAAAAAAAAN! Is that even funny anymore?

I was at the bookstore the other day and I saw a book called "100 Legendary Knives". If you are going to write a book on legendary knives and you expect people to take you seriously I feel it is pretty much unconscionable to have stupid things like bowie knives in there but leave out Sting, or a tooth from Shai-Hulud[1].

Dorothy is wearing a puffy safari shirt and a bad attitude towards authority. Blanche is wearing her "The Real Ghostbusters" outfit. Rose wins the outfit battle, AGAIN.

I don't know what it is about this outfit that makes me think that Blanche has just come from a big breakdancing competition. Which is just silly, because we already discussed how Sophia is the breakdancing master, not Blanche.

This is the way I feel about that "Twitter" thing that people are so keen about these days. Why are you telling the world all these things about your life? Why do you seem to think that everything is just a huge reality TV show?

They just opened up a bunch of packs of Fallen Empires[2] and saw the rares they got.

Another rare kitty appearance. It is hard to believe that in a house of four ultra-centarians, there is not a single pet cat. The cat in the photo looks like my dead friend Zelda, and that is a harsh blow to my "don't cry" shield.

I am not that big of a fan of long-haired cats (at least compared to their short-haired brethren), but I am not going to hold it against Rose that she seems to be enjoying this one. Cats in general tend to be pretty good so I am going to look on the postive side and commend her taste in species rather than being nitpicky about the length of hair.

Welcome back, Dorothy purple joker top. Blanche's harem pants are no match for the horizontal AND vertical stripe dress that Sophia has disturbed our realities with. Try to find her legs in this photo, they are eerily non-existent.

Sophia is wearing a snazzy dress. I am digging the severity of the lines. I tip my bonnet to you, Sophia.

A rare outfit victory for Dorothy. Sensible cotton pants with slip-ons beat billowly shirt with heels...and 50% off Hallmark wrapping paper dress. I am just sitting here looking at pictures of old ladies and making fun of the way they dress. Weak.

Blanche is sad because this is the last one. Don't be sad Blanche. I'll miss you too, but in time our hearts will heal, and we will find new zines to fill the emptiness that lingers.

Endnotes

Preface

1   My favorite example of this is announcers for the Olympics. They are always going on about "They are going so fast they are literally on fire right now!" and "He is literally a laser beam of precision". I think it should be a requirement that if you are a sportscaster that you have some understanding of the difference between metaphor and reality.

Episode I

1   Furries are people that think they are an animal trapped in a human body. I'm all for folks doing what they want with their own lives, but these people are totally gross. They basically sexualize childhood cartoon characters, and make unholy love while wearing elaborate suits designed to make themselves look like their spirit animal.

2   I'm not much for sports...but hockey is, and always will be, awesome. A "hat trick" is when a single player scores three goals in a single game. Go Red Wings.

Incorrect! Go Sabres. (Incorrect about the Red Wings thing. Your hat trick definition is valid).

3   Back in Rochester I used to live in a nudist house. I was not a nudist myself. My bff Evan, his dad is like a senator of nudism and would allow the naturist society of Rochester to come over and use the pool and

hot tub and sauna he illegally built in his basement. They would definitely disapprove of this comment, because they prefer the term topfree to topless. I am taking a big risk on potentially alienating our nude fanbase. However if the movie Strictly Ballroom has taught me anything it's that a life lived in fear is a life half-lived.

4   Deerhoof is a sort of turdy band that a lot of people in Portland seem to be into. Whatever. Steer clear of bands with the word "deer" and "bear" in them.

I am a big fan of Deerhoof, but they are definitely on my list of things I like that I never recommend to other people.

5   I have a huge problem with people that overuse abbreviations. "Urban" is sometimes used in reference to the store "Urban Outfitters"...which is basically "Hot Topic" for yuppies.

6   New Seasons is an Oregon-based "health food"-ish supermarket. It is FANTASTIC. You can buy organic-holistic-meat free meat, but you can also pickup Skippy peanut butter. Everything there is WAY cheaper than Whole Foods too. Love it.

7   Rotture is this club in Portland that people are really keen on. Going there makes me feel really uncomfortable. They have two pinball machines, but neither of them really work. Yeah right, dudes.

I like Rotture, although I have never been there. They are located above the store where I would play in Magic the Gathering tournaments. They were supposed to wait until the tournaments were over before playing music but they never would. I usually enjoyed the music they played but it just annoyed everyone else. Advantage: me.

8   My idea for this came from a contest I had once with a friend. We had heard that it was impossible to drink a gallon of milk in an hour without vomiting, so we decided to try. He opted for the fast and furious approach, while I took slow and steady. He was at about the three quarters mark when he started vomiting. Let me tell you, it was pretty intense. It was like when a firehose gets loose and starts spraying everywhere, and it went on for far longer than you can imagine. It was one of the most hilariously disgusting things I have ever seen, and I cannot encourage you enough to trick other people into trying this.

Incidentally, I do have an idea for how this challenge might be possible. The problem is that the body cannot process the lactose quickly enough. But what if you were a normal lactose tolerant person and you took a bunch of Lactaid first? It might bestow upon you superhuman levels of tolerance for lactose!

Just like when Takashi took the "trichloromethaline" before the tricycle race!

Episode II

1   After the craft store ended my mom got working for Lego. You know what the coolest possible job is for your mom to have when you're a ten year old boy? Working for Lego. My mom: 1; your mom: 0

2   D6 is geek shorthand for six-sided dice. Other common ones are four, eight, ten, twelve and twenty-sided dice. They are important for simulating various degrees of probability when you are playing nerd games.

A popular joke at my high school D&D sessions was to give someone the middle finger and call it a "D1"...not very funny.

3   If nothing else good comes from working on this zine, at least I learned the word "lanai". I am sure it will come in useful in some future game of Scrabble.

BONUS points, it has an anagram...LIANA.

4   The Ace Hotel is a chain of Ikea-Urban Outfitter inspired hotels. If I ever meet someone that loves me, I'd probably spring for a night at this place...to wow them. People do that, right? Is that weird?

Episode III

1   Fort Knox is where the US Treasury stores a large part of their gold reserves. When I was little it was as far as I knew the most securely defended building in the world, and therefore awesome. When you are of a certain age the most or -est of anything is the pinnacle of awesome. Diplodocus? Awesome. Olympus Mons? Awesome. Peregrine Falcon? Awesome. Although now that I think of it all of those things are still pretty great.

2   Ratatat is actually a pretty cool band based out of New York or something. You probably already know what their deal is, so this footnote is weird. One of their songs sounds exactly like the music in Gauntlet...and that gives them a lifetime pass, in my book.

3   This is not true at all.

4   This was easily the best weapon you could find in the Sega Genesis version of Jurasic Park.

5   Police Squad is the TV show that the Naked Gun movies are based on. When I was a kid I would spend the weekends at my dad's house, and we would stop by the movie rental store on the way and we would get a video. I do not think I have enough fingers and toes to count the number of times I made my dad rent this movie.

6   Vice Magazine is the Magazine equivalent of that kid in your high school who made fun of everyone...and you thought he was sort of funny, but you were super scared that he was going to pick on you next. There are a lot of topless ladies in this Magazine.

Episode IV

1   If you don't know that hoverboards were made popular in the 1989 classic, "Back to the Future Part II", then our business with each other has concluded. The rumor referenced here was created by the film's DIRECTOR, Robert Zemeckis. I remember it coming up a couple different times in elementary/middle school, so, it had legs.

2   Foreigner was that 80's band that did Hot Blooded and Cold as Ice and Jukebox Hero and I Wanna Know What Love Is and a lot of other songs that you probably recognize. Whenever I look at their catalog I am constantly surprised by the number of popular songs they have.

3   Here is the deal with kinesiology: lets say they are trying to figure out if a particular kind of food is good for your digestion. They will have you hold the food in your mouth, or maybe some weird pill that has the essence of the food. Then you stick one arm out and they try to push down on it while you resist their pushing. Your body will "know" if the food is good or not, and if it is bad for you it will weaken your body allowing them to push further. It is super easy to fake results, and the whole discipline is pretty worthless unless you are trying to get hot

moms to touch your arm.

4   The possibility that someone reading this would not know who Robocop is really freaks me out. But Robocop is a 21 year old movie, so it is entirely plausible that someone reading this could not even have been born yet when that movie was released. Holy christ that makes me feel old. Note to young people reading this: you are too young and should age significantly.

Anyways, Robocop was a movie about a cop in the future who is basically killed so they make him into a cyborg. It is an action movie but also a treatise on the dangers of corporate influence on government. Between this and Running Man it was a pretty popular theme for science fiction action movies in the eighties. What?! You haven't heard of that one either?! Fuck you, young people!

A few days after writing the preceding paragraph I encountered an eighteen year old and asked him if he had ever heard of Robocop. He answered in the affirmative, that he had watched it as a little kid. I told him I was working on a zine and was concerned that some of the references I was making, references that seemed completely reasonable to me, might now be too dated for some of our younger readers. We talked for awhile about the ability of tv shows and movies to stay in the cultural hive-mind for long after they've been aired. Eventually he asked me what the zine was about it. I told him it was commentary on the outfits of the Golden Girls. He responded with "Who are the Golden Girls?". Kids these days....

5   The Tube is a pretty gross bar in Portland that people like to go to and eat cheap, vegan food. This bar looks like the morning AFTER a really fun party in Neo Tokyo...when the lights turn ON, and everything looks plastic in a gross sort of way. The bathrooms are top notch...but I can't, in good conscious, pee in there knowing how many lines of coke will later be snorted off the toilet seat.

6   This arrangement of dimensions is necessary for superstring theory to work, which is why I think superstring theory is a lot of hooey. Seriously physics dudes, if you need to come up with a bunch of bullshit invisible unprovable dimensions to get things to work then it is time for a new theory. Otherwise you might as well say "God created the universe" and call it a day.

Episode V

1   Gorgons are female monsters in Greek mythology that could turn you to stone if you looked at them. You know Medusa? She was a gorgon.

2   But isn't that basically what you do now?

3   Again, I am lying. A fairly reliable way to tell if I am lying is if I finish with the words "True story".

4   The now bankrupt Mervyns was a then (1990's) shopping powerhouse. Their "deal" is that they had a really cheap looking store...so they were able to keep prices down by labeling it a "no frills" shopping environment. Nice try, dudes. My mom used to buy all my clothes from this place...so I have a lot of memories of walking around it while reading video game instruction manuals.

5   "I'm Too Sexy" by Right Said Fred

6   When you take karate, they tell you to yell this word outloud to focus your "chi"...so you can break a board. Try yelling it when you do things like open a door for your girlfriend...instant fun.

7   Sophia = Ravenclaw, Blanche = Slytherin, Rose = Hufflepuff

8   Action Slacks are a cut/design of pants from the Levi company. They are marketed as dress pants that never wrinkle/crease/letyoudown. My roommate (and various other dudes) got really excited about buying them over the summer. It was basically the only thing we talked about. Eventually, we all got our Action Slacks in the mail (they are notoriously hard to find on the shelf). At first, there was a lot of celebration...the Action Slacks were awesome. However, something never quite sat well with me. Upon further thought and examination, I realized that they are just "warm ups" that have pockets sewn into them. So...they are sort of the "gym person"'s dress pant. I have not been able to wear my Action Slacks since then...and my friends and I never discuss it anymore.

9   A really labored Final Fantasy VI reference that I included solely for the benefit of my friend Evan, who insists that this is the best game ever made. Please note that I prefer the correct, Japanese numbering system for my Final Fantasy games.

10   The "Wrangler Shirt" is an invention of the Levi company. Originally, I think cowboys wore it. I'm not totally sure, but that's what cigarette ads of the 60's and 70's have shown me. In recent years though, the image has been repossed by "hip culture"...and now you'll see kids of all ages walking around with pearl buttons creeping up their chest. For the record, I'm OK with it.

11   My first thought was perhaps they are wearing adult diapers underneath their double robes so that they don't need to worry about having easily removable clothes like tear-away pants and the like. They just pee in bed then change in the morning. However I can tell you from experience that peeing in an adult diaper is not fun, at least not if there is a lot of pee. I have found they are not nearly as absorbent as one would hope. Walking around,

genitalia adrift in a pool of urine, desperately hoping that the seal against your legs does not fail. No thanks!

Episode VI

1   "Parker Lewis Can't Lose" was this TV show from the early nineties that was a complete "Ferris Bueller" ripoff...and didn't even try to cover that up really. The guy that played Parker Lewis would later go on to record a hip-hop album called "Starship of Foolz". That really made me mad...

2   Again, I can't believe I would need to explain this but Double Dragon is a side-scrolling brawler (or "beat-em-up") arcade game, later ported to the NES. Seriously kids, it's like you have no sense of history at all. Let me guess, you haven't heard of Bad Dudes or Streets of Rage either? Oh man! That reminds me of something I haven't thought about in years! It probably comes as no surprise that when I was a little kid I was a huge nerd and not at all popular with the ladies. And it's not like I was ugly, I was just a dorky little momma's boy. So once I was in a pizzeria playing Bad Dudes and there were two girls watching me. This was probably the first time in my eleven of so years of life that a girl had paid interest in me for a reason other than to express disdain. I knew the stakes were high, and the only way I could hope to impress them was by showing off some serious skills against the evil DragonNinja clan. Unfortunately I got a little bit too into the game and when delivering the killing blow against the first boss I actually yelled out "Hi-YA!". The girls laughed at me, and thus I had blew my only opportunity for the next five years to have a girl like me.

That is a killer story. I have a similar, but darker one. I was also a dorky little mama's boy that had no chance with girls. So, I was at this arcade one time (Tilt, at Lakeside Mall), and these two girls were checking me out (I think). Anyway...I'm really deep into Teenage Mutant

Ninja Turtles...and I figure my only way to impress them is to play through the level without getting hit. Things are going great. After a time, I feel someone GRABBING MY ASS. Seriously, no lie. I didn't know what to do...so I just went eyes forward. After a few seconds, I looked over...and realized that the girls were at the other side of the arcade. An impossible distance to grab my ass and then retreat to. SO, I looked over my other shoulder...and who is 10 feet away, smiling like a crazy person? A 40 year old-ish bald man. This was the ass grabber. I spent the next three years alternating between depression and confusion.

That is hilarious and sad but also pretty hilarious. Do you remember that game show where they would get kids playing video games against each other and the one that did the best got to run through a fake video game store grabbing games? It came on at like 6am where I lived but I would wake up early every morning to watch it and just stare at the screen in hatred. Because 90% of the time the game they were playing was the Nintendo version of the TMNT arcade game, and I was so much better at it than those kids were. Those kids were FUCKING UNWORTHY of being on tv. Plus when they won they would spend like the entire minute running around the store looking for the one game they wanted rather than just piling up with as much as they could carry and then just selling it later. Anyways, the arcade TMNT game will always remind me of that show.

3   I feel like you probably shouldn't have had to read the footnote on this one, but I'll explain this anyway. The Emperor's Royal Guard (also known as the Imperial Guard) are these guys in red robes and cool helmets that stand around the Emperor of the Galactic Empire and hold onto cool looking spears. You never really see them do anything in the movies, but they've been used as "mini-boss" type characters in many a Star Wars video game. I could sit here and talk about these guys all day. They are trained to FIGHT TALK with each other using a rare variant of the Echani fighting style...they have limited access to the dark side of the force...no one knows their names...

etc etc etc.. I'M NOT saying that I think the Galactic Empire was a positive element in the Star Wars Universe...but I do admire their command structure, and think their outfits were FAR superior to the Rebellion's.

4   If you do not know what Slaughterhouse Five is, I don't think there is much I can do for you.

Episode VII

1   "The Bins", or formally, "The Goodwill Bins" are a series of warehouse facilities where Goodwill Industries sends all the stuff that doesn't sell in their stores. This stuff is then thrown into a number of large rolling dumpsters (known as bins) and put out onto the floor for unwashed people to furiously rifle through, and purchase by the pound. I love the bins, a lot of people love the bins. It's one of the few places on earth that the "young and hip" mingle with the "middle-aged and earnest" and have non-judgemental battles over clothing.

2   The day that my mom bought me the King's Mountain Fortress with the drawbridge and the trapdoor and the glow-in-the-dark ghost was seriously one of the happiest days of my life.

        I used to set mine up next to the Ewok Village and have space lego guys fight stormtroopers from inside the fortress. It made absolutely no sense.

3   Both characters from the McDonaldland advertising campaign. According to Wikipedia the guy who did The Grimace also voiced Nibbler on Futurama and 8 of 14 Decepticons for the Transformers cartoon. On one hand I can't help but marvel at how the internet has changed the way we interact with information, but on the

other hand I wonder why I care about either of those things.

4   The Doug Fir is this place in Portland that you have to go to if you want to see a mid-level popularity band perform...a band that is too popular to play at a house show, but not popular enough to have a music video on MTV. If they are on MTV, it'll be in the form of background music for an exciting sequence of events on "The Real World". This band MAY also provide background music during segments of "This American Life"...but will almost definitely be too popular to be the segue on "Market Place". Anyway, the Doug Fir blows, but I don't get out too often...so I'm more apt to judge these places harshly.

5   Piranha plants and warp pipes will forever be married in my brain due to a little game called Super Mario Bros. Remember those red bitey things that would pop out of that nice shade of green piping just as you were about to land on top of it? Well, that's a piranha plant coming out of a warp pipe. Deal with that.

6   Here, I am referring to Judge Elihu Smails. The guy who played Judge Smails is the guy that says "Meanwhile, at the Hall of Justice..." on the old Superfriends cartoon. Consider your life enriched.

7   I HAVE to assume that you KNOW who Venom is, the large Spider-Man looking character from the Marvel Universe that wears the black Spider-Man looking outfit. That guy. Anyway, you might not be hip to Carnage, as he is sort of a "comics only" dude. He is basically the red version of Venom, but a little bit meaner. Interesting thing to note though, Carnage was created by the writers to kill off Venom...but Venom was so popular by the time the Carnage books came out,

Marvel wouldn't allow the killing to occur. So, Venom sort of defeated Carnage in real life...with numbers. This may be the only time in your life that you will ever read or think about Carnage. I think that's sort of weird.

8   From the episode where Homer, Otto, Apu and Moe form a bowling team with money that Homer embellezles from Mr. Burns when he is doped up on ether.

9   Considering how the other day I masturbated to the idea of coming home to breakfast having already been made for me, yeah, that does sound pretty wonderful.

10   The unholy trinity of goth music, and don't let anyone else tell you otherwise. The Sisters of Mercy were the nice ones, with some band floor hits, and a later defection to trance music (I once drove all the way to Chicago to see them in concert, only to be shocked and saddened to see that the lead singer had dyed his hair white...and was playing trance music). Led by Peter Murphy, Bauhaus was the thinking man's group...and I wasn't alive when they were popular, but I'm guessing that a lot of people started listening to them because of David Bowie. This band would later spawn the not even close to nearly as good "Love and Rockets". Finally, Christian Death, the mean ones. These guys sang about stuff WAY darker than anything else ever (except for black metal products), and provide great music for teenagers to freak their parents out with.

Episode VIII

1   I wasn't going to tell this story but the zine is a few pages short, so here we go. This took place when I was living in the nudist house with Evan. We were hanging out with our friend Larry when Evan announced that he

was tired, he was gonna pee, then go to bed. Larry exclaims "I WILL GIVE YOU TWENTY DOLLARS TO PEE ON ZACH RIGHT NOW." We pause to consider the offer, then start PURELY THEORETICALLY discusing the logistics of how and where we might accomplish this. After lengthy debate we decide that the best place to do it would be the party shower in the basement that the nudists use to rinse off when using the facilities.

At this point Larry admits that he does not actually have twenty dollars in his budget devoted to voyeuristic watersports. I ask him how much he would pay, he says five bucks. Now as I am sure you will agree, five dollars is not nearly enough money for getting peed on. I tell him that if he PURELY THEORETICALLY BUT MAYBE A LITTLE LESS SO THAN BEFORE would want to make this happen he needs to sweeten the deal. Haggling ensues and eventually a compromise is struck: Evan will pee on me, pro bono. I will get peed on from the neck down, recieve five dollars, and get to pee on Larry's legs. Larry gets nothing other than the pleasure of watching me get peed on. Thus our faustian bargain was struck.

So, it happens. Evan pees on me, and it is no big deal. I pee on Larry and he is DISGUSTED. He claims my urine smells like "rotting bark" and spends the entire time gagging and dry heaving. We both rinse off, he gives me five bucks, and we call it a night. The next day he finally comes to realize that he got a horrible deal. He was pissed on AND had to give me money. He is scarred from the experience and from this day forward acts as a man possessed. We always played a lot of Scrabble and had constant ongoing best-of-39 tournaments. Our wagers used to be creative and diverse but from this point forward his is always the same: he wants his revenge. He wants to piss on me. But the story doesn't end there!

Eventually he gets his wish. Not at Scrabble, but after one of the most inspiring come-from-behind rallies at Super MarioKart battle mode that the world has ever seen (first to 15, I was up 14-2). We go down into the basement, I take off my pants and just stand there while he pisses on my legs. But the experience is anticlimatic for him! I don't react, he gets no thrill! His piss-lust is still unsatiated. He starts trying to pee on our other friends as well, putting it up versus cash in games of Texas hold-em. Not long after, he is victorious against our friend Ben. Ben's requirement is that Larry can only piss on his legs; Ben wants to keep his underwear on so Larry has to be very careful not to get any on his underwear. At this point their stories diverge. Larry claims that during the act Ben was doing a jig, and it was the dancing that caused the stream to get dangerously high. Ben claims that it was Larry just being an asshole and trying to piss on his underpants. Regardless, the end result is the same. Ben grabs at Larry's dick to try and get him to stop, Larry freaks out, and piss starts going everywhere. It is like in Ghostbusters how you are not supposed to cross the streams. They both end up getting sprayed, it is a big mess, and at long last Larry has had enough of peeing on his friends. That is the story of why I am good at Scrabble.

Episode IX

1   A fun experiment: find your nearest American Apparel store. See if they have a bike rack out front. If they do, check in on them several times throughout the day. Make notes on if there are any bikes locked up out front, and if so are any of them fixed gear. Calculate the likelihood of there being a fixed gear bicycle parked out front at any given time. There is no point to this other than to help you feel superior to fixie-riding douchebags who shop at American Apparel.

2   Marilyn Manson's ex-wife. I never really understood this lady. I think she is supposed to be "next level sexy", but I don't see it. I think she is just a ploy to get heavier girls that identify as goth to forever hate themselves. She had a "birth mark" surgically added to her body, and is the new model for the Wonderbra. Yeah, right.

3   Medieval Times is a totally awesome "wizards and warriors" themed restaurant where you go and pay $40 to eat with your hands and watch people beat the crap out of each other on horse

back. I haven't been there in a long time, but I remember feeling like it was a place that I never ever wanted to leave...and actually chocking back some tear fluids when I exited the building into the cold wind of reality.

4   Indiana Jones and the Last Crusade...duh. You know, find Jesus' dirty wine mug...drink it up, live forever...find someone else's dirty wine mug, face Meltsville.

Episode X

1   Lord of the Rings, DUH. The party accidentally awakens a Balrog, an ancient demon of hate and fire. Gandalf holds it off on a narrow bridge above a bottomless void so the others can escape, but is pulled down into the darkness as a result. Guaranteed to get me choked up when I watch the movie. Lame normal people have Rose and Jack clinging to the wreckage of the Titanic, I have Gandalf and Frodo and the Mines of Moria.

Episode XI

1   Jar Jar Binks is basically the figurehead of the downfall of the Star Wars institution. Since he showed up, essentially anything with those two beautiful words stamped on it has been absolutely terrible. You know this guy...he's the animated one that falls down a lot and says "Meesa" instead of "I". I just don't even get it...I wanted to get it for a really long time, but I absolutely do not even get it.

2   "Sniping" is when someone on ebay sits there at their computer and waits until the very last second to put a bid in on a cool item, effectively stealing it away from you without a chance for

retort. People get mad at other people for sniping, but I tend to look at them with reverance. They wanted this thing more than I wanted this thing...so...that's capitalism, right? Is that capitalism?

3   Throne of Bone: Poly Artifact, one colorless mana. 1: Any black spell cast by any player gives you one life.

4   Burning Man is a giant week-long party in the Nevada desert populated by experimental artists and other fuckups. Lots of people I know who I otherwise trust the judgment of tell me that it is a good time, but spending a week surrounded by fire dancers and drum circles sounds like my own personal vision of hell.

Agreed. I consider Burning Man to be the exact opposite of what we're trying to achieve with this zine.

Episode XII

1   Vulcans are those guys from Star Trek with the ears and no emotions. You know, Spock? Love that guy. When I was a child, I had a poster of Spock in my room, and I decied that I was going to live a life as close to his as I could. I failed. It is my personal theory that people with Asperger's Syndrome are actually Vulcans. No one cares that I have this theory, and I've gained nothing from it except personal satisfaction.

2   The Tomahawk Jam is not only the zenith of basketball slam dunks, but is also the most powerful and "in your face" move in all of sports. To perform this move, you just jump up really high in the air, pull your arm to the limit of its extension, and then you just slam it down into the hoop

really quickly. The trick here is judging the amount of distance your fully extended arm needs to slam successfully into the basket. Glorious.

3   From the Simpsons episode where they visit Australia to apologize for Bart making prank calls. That joke is itself a reference to the Crocodile Dundee movies. Meta!

4   You know I am having a tough time coming up with commentary when I resort to copy/pasting the lyrics to Psychadelic Furs songs.

5   Here is my problem with your purse supposition: you are assuming that people carry purses because they are practical. I used to have a circular bright yellow vinyl purse where one side of it was clear plastic, and it had a compartment where you could put a clock in it. Like a full sized wall clock. And that purse was absolutely incredible for starting up conversations about Flava Flav. So you see, sometimes people have ulterior motives for carrying around purses that cannot be explained with your cold Vulcan logic.

6   Fruits is a Japanese street fashion magazine. A photographer walks around the streets of Tokyo taking pictures of young people dressed up all crazy. It contains nothing but their pictures, names, ages, and where they bought each item of clothing. It is good thing to use if you need visual evidence of why Japanese people are crazy, and you want that evidence in a format that is perusable while defecating.

Episode XIII

1   Wait, no, I think that is a monsignor outfit. Shit.

2   The Cell is a movie by the guy who directed REM's "Losing My Religion" video. He also made the movie "The Fall", which I thought was awesome. One of my favorite movies to come out last year. Anyways, The Cell has really beautiful crazy surreal images intercut with an awful detectives-looking-for-a-serial-killer movie. If you haven't seen it, it is almost certainly worth watching as long as you are making heavy use of the fast forward button and are maybe on drugs.

3   "Saw" is a series of movies that are basically snuff films where no one dies. I spent my childhood watching Fangoria's "top 100 most gory movies of all time", and even I think these films are stupid. These films are for people that like Slayer, even though the guys in it are Nazis.

Episode XIV

1   I am pretty sure this is the dude who played the annoying neighbor on Empty Nest. It is weird that despite the fact that EN is a spinoff of GG this guy is playing a different character.

2   I was really torn in trying to decide which of the two big Portland thrift stores to mention, Buffalo Exchange or Red Light. On one hand, Buffalo Exchange is a much larger chain, so readers who are not from Portland will be more likely to get the Buffalo Exchange joke. On the other hand I feel like Red Light is more ludicrously expensive, plus they have always been assholes to me. Fuck you Red Light! Don't be assholes!

3   The Big Rock Candy Mountain is what is classically identified as a "hobo's idea of paradise". It originated from a song in the 1930s, and doesn't really make a lot of sense to me, but I like to say it.

4   Entropy is a pretty important concept in physics. The second law of thermodynamics states that when matter and energy change states (i.e. matter turns into energy or vice versa) you cannot break even in the exchange, you have to lose a little bit in the process. The endpoint of this is that as the universe gets older it also gets cooler, since we are slowly running out of energy. Thermodynamics is great and all, but I really haven't found much application for this knowledge in my life other than it allowing me to understand certain jokes on the show Futurama that might otherwise have gone over my head.

Episode XV

1   "Fixie" is slang for a fixed-gear bike, as opposed to "normal" variable gear bikes. The differences are a) You cannot change gears on a fixed gear bike b) They are usually lighter c) They are easier to maintain as they have fewer parts d) when the rear wheel is in motion your pedals will always be in motion (you cannot coast) and e) it is pretty common for fixed gear bikes to not have any brakes. Riding a fixed gear bike is very much a fashion statement, and in my eyes that statement is "I enjoy looking like a douchebag hipster".

2   He directed a bunch of westerns, many of which prominently feature Clint Eastwood being a badass.

3   B.U.M. Equipment was a clothing line geared towards teenagers that focused on high quality sweatpants and sweatshirts. The rich kids at my school had them. Maybe the rich kids at your school had them too? Did you know that B.U.M. stands for "Body Utility Maintainance"? Not so cool now, are you, rich kids?

Nope. The rich kids sportswear of choice at my school was Umbro.

4   A tachyon is a theoretical subatomic particle that travels faster than light, and therefore kinda sorta maybe can go backwards through time. Or at least that was my understanding of how they work from the Star Trek: The Next Generation series finale when Picard uses the tachyon pulses to accidentally rip open subspace.

5   It is man's nature to meet other men on the field of combat. There's no way around this fact of nature. So, when you are ill-equipped to fight people in real life, you have to fight them in a video game. Capcom is a video game company that has been facilitating this service for nerds since the 1990s.

"This is a war universe. War all the time. That is its nature. There may be other universes based on all sorts of other principles, but ours seems to be based on war and games." Thanks, William S Burroughs! Thanks, "The King of Kong"!

Episode XVI

1   Jet Grind Radio was a game that took place in futuristic Japan and had you somehow use graffiti to support pirate radio and fight against an oppressive government regime. While rollerblading (naturally). It was a good game that looked cool and had a sweet soundtrack.

2   A bag of holding is a Dungeons and Dragons item that allows the player to store a near infinite amount of items inside a pouch roughly the size of a man purse. Although D&D has an incredibly detailed "weight you are allowed to carry" system, nearly every Dungeon Master that has ever put on his robe and rolled some d20s just gives his players this item so he doesn't have to deal with it.

Miami, You've Got Style

3   What the old man says to you when he gives you the wooden sword at the beginning of The Legend of Zelda. It is also featured prominently in a popular LOLcat.

4   Brian Peppers is a guy with Crouzon syndrome that became internet famous when his picture showed up in a sex offender database. He looks "shocking" and because of this, people feel they are allowed to make fun of him all they want. Not cool...but his mention is in this zine for comedic purposes, so, guilty as charged.

5   Laura Ingles Wilder is one of the main characters in the series of "Little House on the Praire" books. This series was adapted into a TV show, and I used to pretend I was sick so I could stay home from school and watch. Nelly is one of the first girls that I remember having a tanglible "crush" on.

6   That is to say, topfree.

7   REI is an "upscale" outdoor clothing store. I'd say about 95% of the people that shop there are weekend warriors, and I say this with the full knowledge that I'm a WANNA-BE weekend warrior. Wait, why is it even a negative thing to be a weekend warrior, and why do I feel like I have to self-depricate to defend against making this judgement?

Episode XVII

1   MMA refers to Mixed Martial Arts, an umbrella term for the K1, Pride, Ultimate Fighting Championship, Sportfight, and a few other leagues. All of which involve two people beating the pudding out of each other. They can be pretty entertaining to watch if you are into that sort of thing, however I feel like they don't really reach their potential. Pretty much everyone participating nowadays just has the same basic fighting style of some boxing, some Thai kickboxing, and some Brazillian ju-jitsu. This could be so much more entertaining if you were pitting people with diverse skillsets against each other. Like a Mishima-style karate dude against a capoiera guy. Or a sumo wrestler versus a yogi mystic who can strech his limbs out really far and breathe fire. Both of those things would be pretty good.

2   "The Real Ghostbusters" was an animated series in the 90s that I watched every morning as a young man. I remember thinking it was sort of dumb, but check it out, it was nominated for Emmy awards...and that used to be sort of a big deal, right?

This show always bothered me, mostly because Slimer was one of the good guys. I had a hard time wrapping my head around that. It is the earliest time I can think of where the obsessive nerd in me was upset by inconsistencies in canon.

3   These are the series of rules that govern business and trade amoungst the Ferengi's (a race of traders in the Star Trek universe). Most of them are pretty dumb, but they are excellent ways to break the ice with the clerk during a transaction at your local video game or comic book store.

Episode XVIII

1   Land of the Lost was a show in the 70s about a family who falls through a dimensional portal into a land with dinosaurs. Or maybe they just go back in time? I am not sure. I did not watch this show, nor the 90's remake. By this point of my life my love of all things dinosaur-related had been spoiled by the TGIF show "Dinosaurs".

2   Klinger was the lovable, crossdressing man from the TV show MASH. He was always trying to cook up a way to be deemed "unfit for duty", and get kicked out of the army. The fact that he went about this by crossdressing is sort of insulting though, and a generation of transgendered men and women probably felt a little weird about the whole thing.

3   Final Fantasy II is a really awesome roleplaying game for the Super Nintendo. It's probably the game that I remember playing the most as a young man. And yes, I seriously did cry…because there is a scene where all these people join together to combat the forces of evil. Even as a child, I was very sensitive to the imbalance of good v. evil in this world.

You totally surprised me here. I expected it to be when Palum and Porem sacrifice themselves.

4   The Jedi Counsel is comprised of the strongest and wisest Jedi Knights in the galaxy. I just wrote that sentence alone…in my basement.

5   Jem was an awesome cartoon from the late 80's about this girl named Jerrica that used holographic powers to create the best all-girl rock outfit of all time, "Jem and the Holograms".

I credit this TV show with solidifying the notion in my 8 year old brain that girls could do cool things too.

I am pretty sure the Misfits were better than the Holograms. I mean, it says so right in their song.

6   A Drudge Skeleton is a 1/1 regenerating black creature with a casting cost of one black and one colourless mana. I just pulled that out off the top of my head. Impressed much? Anyway, it's a card from that card game "Magic the Gathering". I was a heavy participant of this game from the ages of 13-17.

7   I am not kidding even a little bit. That video is so fucking great. I think I will go watch it right now!

Episode XIX

1   Seriously. To everyone who hangs your toiletpaper underhand, what the fuck is wrong with you? Do you enjoy making it hard for people to wipe their bottoms?

2   I instantly recognized this dude as being the villain in the Weird Al Yankovich movie UHF. That was the first movie I ever thought was funny enough to buy myself a copy of. Plus according to IMDB he was also in an episode of Mathnet, which officially makes him King Shit of Fuck Mountain in my book.

Episode XX

1   From the Simpsons episode where Homer and Mr. Burns get trapped in the cabin together. At the peak over 13% of my neural capacity was given over to memorized Simpsons dialogue.

2   Quake was a computer game manufactured by Id software, also known for such timeless classics as Wolfenstein and Doom. It introduced the ability to look up and down, and therefore made it impossible for me to play any future game in the genre without getting horribly motion-sick.

3   Salieri was the bad guy in the movie Amedeus, but probably not that much of a douchebag in real life.

4   As previously mentioned there are lots of different dice used to determine probability in Dungeons and Dragons (as well as other tabletop RPGs). Let's say you have a Longsword that has +2 orc slaying. Normally you would say you're going to attack the orc, and then you roll a d20, and if you get a 13 or higher your attack would hit. But with a sword that has +2 orc slaying, you add 2 to the die roll. So in this case an 11 or higher is all you would need to hit. That is what I am referring to with this one.

5   Empty Nest was a TV show that aired immediately after the Golden Girls for a period on NBC...there are even crossover episodes with the G Girls. It's not that good of a show, but there's a big dog on it named Dreyfuss, and it's hard to stay angry with an unfair world when there's a big dog smiling at you.

6   Thing is the disembodied hand from The Addam's Family. I will admit that I had to look

this up online, but I think it's sort of a cool thing to share...Thing was played by the hand of the actor that portrays Lurch. Why do I even care about this? ....I do.

7 Donatello was always my favorite Ninja Turtle, and not only because he was the smart nerdy one who I could identify with. Sure, Leo has two katana which IN THEORY is way better than a bo staff. However because it was a kids show he never really got to use them to their full potential. All he could do was use them to pick up garbage cans then throw them over the heads of Foot Soldier robots. As opposed to Donatello, who could beat on people with his staff to his hearts content because bashing damage is more acceptable for kids to see than cutting or piercing (hidden D&D reference for all you nerds out there!)

I officially became "gay" for you after reading that last statement. Is that weird?

8 The Silver Age of comics refers to the period between 1956 and the early 70's. During this period, the Joker was usually presented as a loud goofball who wore really garish shirts...a far cry from the Heath Ledger Joker of aught eight.

Episode XXI

1 This is another reference to Magic the Gathering. Trample is an ability that allows creatures to direct any points of damage remaining from combat with another creature over to the opposing spellcaster. I will never find a wife.

2 The SCA, or Society of Creative Anachronism, is a group of dorks for whom going to the renaissance faire is not enough. These are the people who put on fake armor and beat on each other with swords

wrapped in foam and pretend that they are living in some weird alternate-universe middle ages where people call each other lord and lady as opposed to lying around covered with feces and lesions all day until they die of smallpox. As a dude who spent his last birthday alone and sitting in the dark watching the Lord of the Ring movies, this should be a pretty great time. However in my experience they do a spectacular job of making it not fun.

3   If you haven't seen "The Seventh Seal", just replace that reference with "Bill and Ted's Bogus Journey".

4   Cobra Kai is the dojo that is filled with all the enemies of the Karate Kid in the Ralph Macchio opus, "The Karate Kid". It's the only small town dojo I've ever heard of that encourages its students to attack and make fun of everyone, and I think that this is sort of a cool thing.

Episode XXII

1   Push Up Pops (not to be confused with Push Pops) are those delightful tubes of sherbet that the ice cream man will sell you for three dollars. The notion of having "control" over how much of the pop is available for consumption must be an appealing thing for a child to have, because so many things are out of their hands in their formative years. Push Up Pop Psychology.

Your ice cream man (or "Skippy" as we called him back east) is ripping you off.

2   Strawberry Shortcake is a cartoon/doll/toy/thing. She wears a strawberry-themed outfit and she has a cat named Custard and a bunch of friends who also have food-themed names. I only remember it from when I was young, but apparently they have tried to relaunch the brand four times since then. I think the most notable thing about her is that she originated as a greeting card line, and is probably the only greeting card character to get her own video game.

3   > what is a grue?

The grue is a sinister, lurking presence in the dark places of the earth. Its favorite diet is adventurers, but its insatiable appetite is tempered by its fear of light. No grue has ever been seen by the light of day, and few have survived its fearsome jaws to tell the tale.

4   David Byrne was the lead singer of the band Talking Heads, and Stop Making Sense was a concert film of them, directed by Jonathan Demme. David Byrne currently sits in the top position on my all time best concerts list, and that show I had horrible stomach cramps the entire time.

Episode XXIII

1   Sorry everyone, I don't care for Holocene either. It's a bar/venue in Portland where people go to dance and dance and dance. I go there to watch people dance, see a thing that I feel like I have to see, and then leave early...having never actually gotten up to the bar for a drink. I'm not as mean and bitter as these things probably make me sound, I just have an aversion to people enjoying themselves in a public setting.

2   Every human being on this planet knows who Chewbacca, hero of Kashyyyk, is...so I won't insult you with that knowledge. You, however, might not be too "up" on the particulars of Chewbacca fashion. He wears a bandolier strap that looks like the thing on the wall.

3   The Kessel Run is from Star Wars. The Millennium Falcon can do it in less than 12 parsecs. I know what you're thinking: a parsec is a measure of distance, not time. Sure, the Millennium Falcon is supposed to be one of the fastest ships in the galaxy but why would that result in a shorter distance traveled? The answer is simple. The Kessel Run skirts an enormous cluster of black holes known as The Maw. The combination of the ship speed and sophistication of the Millennium Falcon's navigational computers allow it to take a more direct route that slower ships. Hence, 12 parsecs.

4   Gondor was founded by brothers Isildur and Anrion, exiles from the downfallen island kingdom of Numenor, and together with Arnor in the north served as last strongholds of the Men of the West...and I refuse to explain this in any more detail.

Episode XXIV

Episode XXV

1   Sting was the name of Bilbo's sword in the Hobbit, later bequeathed to Frodo in The Fellowship of the Ring. A Shai-Hulud is a species of sandworm native to the planet Arrakis, from the Dune series by Frank Herbert. I was surprised at how hard it was to come up with famous knives from fantasy literature! Everyone has a big hard-on for swords I guess. Everywhere I looked it was Icingdeath this and Glamdring that.

2   I make fun of it here, but I think Fallen Empires is super underrated! Think about it! Goblin Grenade, Order of the Ebon Hand, Order of Leitbur, High Tide, Hymn to Tourach, Icatian Javelineers. All tournament worthy cards at one point or another! Sure the hominids were shitty, but thrulls and thallids more than made up for them, and the whole set had kickass art and flavor text. The only problems with the set was that they made too many packs, and all the best cards were commons. But when if comes to percentage of overall playable cards in the set, go crack open a few packs of Homelands or The Dark or even Legends and tell me how much chaff you get. We'll see how much you look down on Fallen Empires after you get Great Wall and Seafarer's Quay as your rare. (I am talking about Magic: The Gathering btw)

Thank you

For Being a Friend!